PAUL VERLAINE

Selected Poems

Verlaine in fall und busse fromm und kindlich . . .

STEPHAN GEORGE, "Franken"

> *Entonces yo soñé,*
> *la canción,*
> *que nunca diré.*
>
> GARCÍA LORCA, "Verlaine"

PAUL VERLAINE

SELECTED POEMS

Translated by C. F. MacIntyre

UNIVERSITY OF CALIFORNIA PRESS
BERKELEY, LOS ANGELES, LONDON

UNIVERSITY OF CALIFORNIA PRESS
BERKELEY AND LOS ANGELES
CALIFORNIA

UNIVERSITY OF CALIFORNIA PRESS, LTD.
LONDON, ENGLAND

ISBN 0-520-01298-4

11   12   13   14   15

PRINTED IN THE UNITED STATES OF AMERICA

THE PAPER USED IN THIS PUBLICATION MEETS THE
MINIMUM REQUIREMENTS OF AMERICAN NATIONAL
STANDARD FOR INFORMATION SCIENCES—PERMANENCE
OF PAPER FOR PRINTED LIBRARY MATERIALS
ANSI Z39.48–1984. ⊗

DÉDIÉ À
L'ORGUEIL DE LA MAISON
TOU-TOU

PREFACE

I

THE LIFE of Paul Verlaine has been dispassionately presented by his friend, Edmond Lepelletier, and the translation by E. M. Lang, *Paul Verlaine: His Life—His Work* (London, T. Werner Laurie), is readily available. Thus the man has been wisely put beyond the reach of the Victorian ghoulishness of Edmund Gosse, George Moore, and Arthur Symons, all of whom loved too well the scrambled legend of "Pauvre Lélian" and his "absinthe-tinted song."

Translations of some of the poems have been done by Symons and by Ernest Dowson. Gertrude Hall (1895), Ashmore Wingate (1905), and Bergen Applegate (1916) have offered book-length versions. All have the merits—and the defects—of the literary jargon of their eras. And we have it on the word of Dryden that any translation is good only for the generation during which it was made.

The poems presented here were taken from the *Œuvres complètes,* Tome I (Paris, Vanier, 1900), which includes Verlaine's first six books of verse. An occasional variant has been taken from *Choix de poésies* (Paris, Charpentier, 1911) and has been cited in the Notes.

As for the form in which I have put these poems: often enough, they have fallen into fairly exact rhymes; but I have not hesitated, when a choice offered of preserving the meaning (as I saw it) or of wrenching the sense to get a more perfect rhyme, to adopt any slant, suspended, or near rhymes, consonances, or assonances which suggested themselves. And I flatly state that an "s" as a plural or verb form does not strike me as anything to be considered. There are too many sibilants in our language. The adjective in French too often falls at the line's end and, naturally, often makes a good rhyme in its English form; but I have tried to keep my versions in a legitimate order as logical as that of good English prose. In an addendum to my *Faust,* Part I, I mentioned the major precepts which should monitor all translation, and these came from acknowledged authorities.

I have needed, and fortunately had, more help and advice with this book than with any other. Gratefully I acknowledge the felicitous aid of Howard Baker, the finesse of Mathurin Dondo, and the extramural assistance (outside of normal working hours) of August Frugé and Harold A. Small of the University of California Press.

II. VERLAINE'S FIRST SIX VOLUMES

Poèmes saturniens, 1866, after a dedication to Eugène Carrière, opens with a prologue in couplets which announces a position that gave a name to the short-lived literary group *Les Impassibles:* the world has exiled the poets, and they have retreated to the ivory tower. Baudelaire had supplied this formula in "Bénédiction" and "L'Albatros." Leconte de Lisle had turned the eyes of the younger poets toward the East and had taught them, as did Gautier, to use a chisel rather than a lute in fashioning their verses. Hugo had loosed an epidemic of rhetoric and bombast, and all the young men contracted the disease. Yet Verlaine had already a voice of his own. Although the poems here are mainly descriptive and objective, the book contains many evidences of the fantasy, the whimsicality, the wistfulness and flippancy, which were later to become his principal characteristics. For instance, he stands the first sonnet on its head (as Baudelaire had taught him), and calmly proceeds in the rest of his work to violate most of his declared tenets. His fine lyric note is as yet restrained in the strait limits of the sonnet or drowned in the couplets of the longer poems. Later, he was to crack the alexandrine into two or three sections. The most famous poem is "Chanson d'automne." Of course, it is untranslatable; yet one must try. "Épilogue," which concludes the volume (because of its length, here summarized in the Notes), condenses the counsels of Boileau, with warnings against the commonplace and inspiration; it recommends "will power," of which the poet had never the faintest conception; study, of which he was incapable; and the "cold chiseling of moving verses," which is like asking a thrush to become a stonemason. But the book as a whole is a remarkable performance for a young man of twenty-two.

The next volume, *Fêtes galantes,* 1869, is a triumph of the *parnassien* theory. The verses are as strict as those of Banville. The subject matter synthesizes the manners of the eighteenth-century nobility as seen in the paintings of Watteau, Fragonard, Boucher, etc. The marquis, the abbé, the coquette, and the stock figures from the Italian comedy are all present, like Dresden figures in a museum at twilight. The atmosphere is silver and silken, and lutes and fountains tinkle prettily. It is all delightfully artificial, a series of colored engravings. But already the future of Verlaine's life is indicated in the final poem:

> Even so they walked through the wild oats, these dead,
> and only the night heard the words they said.

Meanwhile the poet fell in love, paid a short but stormy courtship, and married. *La Bonne Chanson,* 1870, marks an abrupt transition from objective, plastic verse to a rapturous, almost factual diary of his relations with Mathilde Mauté. He has fallen pell-mell from his tower and can make poems about the Parisian streets through which he travels toward "paradise," and the friendly, intimate hours by the hearth; he takes pleasure in describing the manners and dresses of a real woman, and the poems are wistful and tender. The book is important as a transition mark, for his poetry was seldom again to be free from the confessional note and from evidences of suffering. The series is not really complete without a consideration of *Birds in the Night* from the next volume, as a melancholy sequel.

In 1874, *Romances sans paroles* presents a full-fledged poet. *Ariettes oubliées,* which make up the first section, are delicate poems of yearning and languor, pathos and sentiment, and they sing as carelessly as birds. The brisk vagabond verses of *Paysages belges,* fresh with the little adventures of the open road which he traveled with his erratic but brilliant companion Arthur Rimbaud, were destined to be reworked in his prison at Mons, after the drunken pot-shot at his friend. *Birds in the Night*—the title was in English—are bitterly ironic regrets and recriminations of his marriage, now broken up. The *Romances* are, in the main, vaguely irritating and yet strangely compulsive poems: their gamut runs from nursery rhymes to the ultimate achievements of French lyricism, from merry-go-rounds to the utter misery of a heart. There is little like them in all poetry save in the sardonic laughter of Villon, the mockeries of Catullus, the irony of Heine, and some of the bitter flippancies of Corbière, whose *Amours jaunes* preceded *Romances sans paroles* by a year. A new, indefinable note had burst, brief as a rocket's fall, eternal as the wailing of the damned. The poet had completely separated himself from his earlier, ordered existence. He had lost his employment, his home, his wife, and his child. He is henceforth—save for the brief interlude of *Sagesse*—bound over wholly to the bohemian life of careless wandering and dissipation. He passes through an endless maze of hospitals, cafés, lawsuits, and quarrels, with another prison or two thrown in. His companions hereafter are the younger idolizing poets and a succession of demi-reps; but his position as a major poet has been assured. Violent perturbations and temptations have made him at least a psychotic, and an alcoholic patient; his body is racked with agony, and his mind is the prey of remorses.

In this mood he was ripe for the spiritual crisis precipitated in the prison at Mons and expressed in *Sagesse,* 1881. One is re-

minded of Plato's "We are as great as the peaks of our desires."
Many of the poems are a spiritual history of his conversion; yet
they are singularly free from versified theological dogma and
from evidences of "cage sickness." He has entirely cast off the
earlier *parnassien* influence, and the poems, even the sonnets,
flow in liquid music. He sings like an ardent Catholic of the
Middle Ages. His very tears become lyrics, and his groans are
turned into chants and hymns. In a minor way, he has written
a little *Divine Comedy* of a simple and contrite heart. These
poems, along with those of Hopkins and Claudel, and Rilke's
Marienleben, constitute perhaps the last great religious docu-
ments in verse that we are likely to experience in our time.
Their sincerity has nothing to do with the fact that he fell from
grace and came to a bad end. Aside from his next book, he was
finished as a great poet.

Of the poems collected in *Jadis et naguère,* 1884, which Huys-
mans in *À rebours* calls "his last volume," some were written in
other periods and some are deliberate imitations of his earlier
styles; hence the book does not have the impact of a unified
production. Although it gives somewhat the effect of an an-
thology by several poets, it contains work well able to stand
alone. Best known perhaps is "Art poétique": "De la musique
avant toute chose ... et tout le reste est littérature." This con-
stituted a springboard from which the Symbolists took the leap
into the azure absolute, so dear to their dreams. Broken in
health, and impoverished by lawsuits, Verlaine had returned to
Paris, to become the hero of the younger poets. Although he
published half a dozen other books of poems, the total worth of
them has not encouraged any serious attempt at translation in
the intervening sixty years. By 1885 he had already become a
faint echo of his poem "A Horatio": "mon doux briseur de pots
... gloire des tripots." He had attained, even in life, the haunting
unreality of his ultimate legend as Pauvre Lélian; but his ana-
grammatic self proved a bad rival to the poet Paul Verlaine.

The reader may never have heard of Verlaine, but not a few of the poems, in particular "Clair de lune" and "En bateau," must have insinuated a musical awareness of the strange new voice into the consciousness of even the radio public because of the setting given them by Debussy; and there may be noted also, among others, the scores for "Colloque sentimental" by Charles Bordes and for "La lune blanche" (under the title "Heure exquise") and parts of *Sagesse* (under the title "D'une prison") by Reynoldo Hahn. Pater might have been writing about Symbolism in general, and about Verlaine in particular, when, in "The School of Giorgione," he said, "All art constantly aspires towards the conditions of music." Not a few painters have sketched or painted portraits of Verlaine; among others, Cazals, Zorn, and Carrière. Degas's "L'Absinthe," alcohol and tart, though not picturing Verlaine, probably best summarizes the physical life of the unhappy poet. Much of the most successful of his poetry has been selected as the text of the present volume. His literary reputation and his fame are left in the care of his only legitimate critics—his compatriots and his artistic peers.

IV. HOMAGE

Of the half-dozen funeral orations delivered at the burial of Paul Verlaine in the cemetery of the Batignolles, in 1896, one by François Coppée has since been used as the preface for *Choix de poésies,* and a paragraph from it contains the essence of any criticism of the poet's work which will have validity down time:

… His name will always awaken remembrance of a poetry absolutely new, which has assumed in French letters the importance of a discovery.

Yes, Verlaine has created a poetry which is indeed his alone, the poetry of an inspiration at once childlike and subtle, entirely of nuances, a poetry evocative of the most delicate vibrations of the nerves, the most fugitive echoes of the heart; a natural poetry, however, springing from a source at times almost popular; a poetry in which the rhythms, free and broken, preserve a delightful harmony, the strophes swirl and sing as in a roundelay of children, and the verses, which yet remain verses—and are among the most exquisite,—are already music. And in this inimitable poetry he has told us all his ardors, faults, remorses, tendernesses, dreams, and has shown us his so troubled yet so ingenuous heart.

Such poems are made to last . . .

The next year, before a group of the poet's friends, Stéphane Mallarmé, in one of his most obscure sonnets, severely separated the man and the poet. Characteristically, and without benefit of proper punctuation, he begins the poem with a rock when he really means a cloud:

TOMBEAU

The black rock angered that the northern blast
rolls it will not be held by pious hands
feeling that for all human ills it stands
to praise some fatal mold whence it was cast.

Usually if the ringdove coos here
this immaterial grief with many a cloud
enfolding hides tomorrow's ripened star
whose scintillations will besilver the crowd.

Who, following the solitary bound,
just now outside, of this our vagabond—
who seeks Verlaine? He is hidden in the grass,

Verlaine but to surprise naïvely at peace
with the lips not drinking nor holding his breath
a so thin stream calumniated: Death.

J.-K. Huysmans, in *A rebours* (chap. xiv), writes that the poet's work was

supplied with rhymes by using verb tenses, sometimes even lengthy adverbs . . . his verse, divided by impossible caesuras, often became singularly obscure because of its bold ellipses and odd violations of the rule which nevertheless gave it a certain charm. He handled meters better than most poets, and tried to rejuvenate stereotyped poetry—for instance, the sonnet which he turned around, tail in the air, like those Japanese fish of motley earthenware which rest gills downward on their pedestals.... He showed a predilection for masculine rhymes ... His individuality was mainly noticeable because he knew how to suggest vague delicious secrets whispered in the dusk. He alone had the art to reveal certain mysterious and disturbing instincts of the heart.... It is no longer the unbounded horizon revealed through unforgettable portals by Baudelaire; it is rather, on a moonlit night, a half-opened chink ... with a view more restricted and intimate, a field peculiar to Verlaine himself.

In one of the crisp, unexpanded essays of *Le Livre des masques,* Rémy de Gourmont has anticipated another belated tribute to the poet:

... To confess the sins of one's actions or dreams is not sinful; no public confession can bring ill fame to any man, for we are all equal and equally tempted, and no one commits a crime of which his brothers are not also capable. That is the reason why the sanctimonious journals and the Academy vainly shamed themselves by abusing Verlaine, silent below the flowers; the kicks of the janitors and the scoundrels have been broken on the pedestal already of granite, and in the meantime, in his beard of marble, Verlaine was everlastingly smiling, like a faun who listens to the ringing of bells.

Paul Valéry, in his essay "Villon et Verlaine," has presented a sadder picture:

How many times I have watched him pass my door, angry, cursing, striking the earth with the heavy stick of a sick man or a threatening tramp! How could one imagine that this vagrant—so brutal in appearance and speech, sordid and yet perturbing and pathetic—could be the writer of the most delicate music in our poetry, of the newest and most disturbing word-melodies in our language?

Today, in a grassplot surrounded by bushes in the southwest corner of the Jardin du Luxembourg, not too far away from his beloved cafés on the Boulevard Saint-Michel, and not too far from the garish little booth of the Punch and Judy show and the quaint undersized merry-go-round, both gay with the shouts and laughter of children whose hearts his own at its best so resembled, the weather-tarnished bust of Paul Verlaine smiles like the old faun in his poem—*rit au centre des boulingrins;* but he had already created for himself a more enduring monument.

◇   ◇   ◇

The proof sheets of this book reach me in Paris, and an emotion seizes me as when one feels like an iron filing under the magnetic great portal of a cathedral. I go up the hill of Clichy to the cemetery of the Batignolles, a small, cozy place surrounded by maples and chestnuts, the latter in full bloom. There is not a grave, however moss-grown and crumbled its stone, which the wind, less forgetful apparently than human beings, has not covered with the small white blossoms with rose-colored centers. It is a warm spring afternoon, and I read all the sheets—without benefit of the imagined ringdoves of Mallarmé, or of any *revenant;* but I get a vast feeling of satisfaction out of cleaning off the name PAUL VERLAINE, POËTE, with some Armagnac: a more pleasing tribute, I dare say, to the old rascal's dust than a bouquet of flowers would be! Death may have been "a so thin stream calumniated" to Mallarmé; yet it seems a very permanent thing, that gray stone under the trees. But I know that under my arm I have a frail part of Verlaine's immortality.

C. F. M.

Paris, 26 avril 1948

CONTENTS

LA BONNE CHANSON—1870

ROMANCES SANS PAROLES—1874

ARIETTES OUBLIÉES

SAGESSE—1881

I

III

III (*Continued*)

JADIS ET NAGUÈRE—1884

JADIS

A LA MANIÈRE DE PLUSIEURS

POÈMES SATURNIENS

1866

MÉLANCHOLIA

❦

I. RÉSIGNATION

Tout enfant, j'allais rêvant Ko-Hinnor,
Somptuosité persane et papale,
Héliogabale et Sardanapale!

Mon désir créait sous des toits en or,
Parmi les parfums, au son des musiques,
Des harems sans fin, paradis physiques!

Aujourd'hui plus calme et non moins ardent,
Mais sachant la vie et qu'il faut qu'on plie,
J'ai dû refréner ma belle folie,
Sans me résigner par trop cependant.

Soit! le grandiose échappe à ma dent,
Mais fi de l'aimable et fi de la lie!
Et je hais toujours la femme jolie!
La rime assonante et l'ami prudent.

MELANCHOLIA

❀

I. RESIGNATION

As a child I dreamt of Persian pomp and show,
Kohinoor and Sardanapalus,
papal state and Heliogabalus!

My longing conjured up vast pleasure-domes
of gold, a paradise, seraglio
filled with the sound of music, and perfumes!

More calm today, although with no less fire,
but knowing life and that one has to bend,
I curb the lovely folly of desire—
without, however, being too resigned.

So be it! The grandiose escapes sometimes;
but away with pleasant things, down with the common!
I always hate the merely pretty woman,
the prudent friend, and the assonantal rhyme.

II. NEVERMORE

Souvenir, souvenir, que me veux-tu? L'automne
Faisait voler la grive à travers l'air atone,
Et le soleil dardait un rayon monotone
Sur le bois jaunissant où la bise détone.

Nous étions seul à seule et marchions en rêvant,
Elle et moi, les cheveux et la pensée au vent.
Soudain, tournant vers moi son regard émouvant:
«Quel fut ton plus beau jour!» fit sa voix d'or vivant,

Sa voix douce et sonore, au frais timbre angélique.
Un sourire discret lui donna la réplique,
Et je baisai sa main blanche, dévotement.

—Ah! les premières fleurs qu'elles sont parfumées!
Et qu'il bruit avec un murmure charmant
Le premier *oui* qui sort de lèvres bien-aimées!

II. NEVERMORE

Memory, memory, what do you want of me?
Autumn drives the thrush down the languid air,
and the sun darts his rays monotonously
on the yellowing woods as the north wind rumbles there.

We were walking in a dream, and we were alone,
she and I, our thoughts like our hair wind-blown.
In her voice of living gold, with that troubling gaze,
she suddenly asked, "Which were your happiest days?"

in her fresh sonorous voice, as an angel's sweet.
Devotedly, to answer her, I bent
and kissed her white hand, with a smile discreet.

—Ah, how the first flowers have the finest scent!
and in a murmur, charmingly, how slips
the first "Yes" from the well-belovèd lips!

III. APRÈS TROIS ANS

Ayant poussé la porte étroite qui chancelle,
Je me suis promené dans le petit jardin
Qu'éclairait doucement le soleil du matin,
Pailletant chaque fleur d'une humide étincelle.

Rien n'a changé. J'ai tout revu: l'humble tonnelle
De vigne folle avec les chaises de rotin...
Le jet d'eau fait toujours son murmure argentin
Et le vieux tremble sa plainte sempiternelle.

Les roses comme avant palpitent; comme avant,
Les grands lys orgueilleux se balancent au vent.
Chaque alouette qui va et vient m'est connue.

Même j'ai retrouvé debout la Velléda,
Dont le plâtre s'écaille au bout de l'avenue.
—Grêle, parmi l'odeur fade du réséda.

III. AFTER THREE YEARS

Pushing the narrow sagging gate aside,
I walked into the little garden-bower
which the sun, that morning, softly glorified,
bespangling with wet sparks the smallest flower.

Nothing had changed. I saw it all: the humble
trellis of wild vine, the rattan chairs . . .
the fountain murmurming its silver air,
the old aspen everlastingly atremble.

Just as they used to be: the quivering rose,
the haughty lily on the wind-swayed stalk.
I still know every lark that comes and goes.

I found the Veleda standing even yet,
her plaster scaling, at the end of the walk—
gracile, in the dull scent of mignonette.

IV. VŒU

Ah! les oaristys! les premières maîtresses!
L'or des cheveux, l'azur des yeux, la fleur des chairs,
Et puis, parmi l'odeur des corps jeunes et chers,
La spontanéité craintive des caresses!

Sont-elles assez loin toutes ces allégresses
Et toutes ces candeurs! Hélas! toutes devers
Le Printemps des regrets ont fui les noirs hivers
De mes ennuis, de mes dégoûts, de mes détresses!

Si que me voilà seul à présent, morne et seul,
Morne et désespéré, plus glacé qu'un aïeul,
Et tel qu'un orphelin pauvre sans sœur aînée.

O la femme à l'amour câlin et réchauffant,
Douce, pensive et brune, et jamais étonnée,
Et qui parfois vous baise au front, comme un enfant.

IV. WISH

Ah, the oaristys! the first mistresses!
The golden hair, blue eyes, the flowering flesh,
and then, in the fragrance of bodies young and fresh,
the timorous spontaneity of caresses!

How far away now all this happiness
and this naïveté; alas, fled back
to the Springtime of regrets from winters black
with my ennui, my loathing and distress!

Now I am here alone, sad and despised,
mournful and helpless, cold as a grandsire,
like an orphan, poor and sisterless.

Oh, the woman coaxing up love's fire,
pensive, sweet and dark, forever surprised,
who sometimes gives your brow a childish kiss.

V. LASSITUDE

A batallas de amor campo de pluma.
GONGORA

De la douceur, de la douceur, de la douceur!
Calme un peu ces transports fébriles, ma charmante.
Même au fort du déduit, parfois, vois-tu, l'amante
Doit avoir l'abandon paisible de la sœur.

Sois langoureuse, fais ta caresse endormante,
Bien égaux tes soupirs et ton regard berceur.
Va, l'étreinte jalouse et le spasme obsesseur
Ne valent pas un long baiser, même qui mente!

Mais dans ton cher cœur d'or, me dis-tu, mon enfant,
La fauve passion va sonnant l'oliphant.
Laisse-la trompetter à son aise, la gueuse!

Mets ton front sur mon front et ta main dans ma main,
Et fais-moi des serments que tu rompras demain,
Et pleurons jusqu'au jour, ô petite fougueuse!

V. LASSITUDE

For battles of love a field of feathers.
GONGORA

Oh, how sweet the sweetness! oh, how sweet!
Calm these feverish raptures a bit; a mistress
should have at the height of pleasure a discreet
abandonment, like the gentle love of a sister.

Be languorous; make lulling your caress,
likewise your soothing glances and your sighs.
No! the obsessive spasm, the jealous embrace
aren't worth a long slow kiss, even one that lies!

Child, in your dear golden heart, you say,
savage Passion winds her clarion.
The hussy, let her trumpet as she may!

Your cheek to mine, and your hand in my hand,
make me those promises you'll break at dawn,
and let us weep till then, my young firebrand!

VI. MON RÊVE FAMILIER

Je fais souvent ce rêve étrange et pénétrant
D'une femme inconnue, et que j'aime, et qui m'aime,
Et qui n'est, chaque fois, ni tout à fait la même
Ni tout à fait une autre, et m'aime et me comprend.

Car elle me comprend, et mon cœur, transparent
Pour elle seule, hélas! cesse d'être un problème
Pour elle seule, et les moiteurs de mon front blême,
Elle seule les sait rafraîchir, en pleurant.

Est-elle brune, blonde ou rousse?—Je l'ignore.
Son nom? Je me souviens qu'il est doux et sonore,
Comme ceux des aimés que la Vie exila.

Son regard est pareil au regard des statues,
Et, pour sa voix, lointaine, et calme, et grave, elle a
L'inflexion des voix chères qui se sont tues.

VI. MY FAMILIAR DREAM

I often have this strange and piercing dream
of a nameless woman—that we love each other;
she loves and understands me; never the same
woman, nor yet at any time another.

She understands me, and my heart grows clear
for her alone—no problem; she knows how
to wipe away the sweat from my pale brow,
and only she can cool it with her tears.

Blonde, auburn, or brunette?—I do not know.
Her name? I remember it is sonorous
and sweet as the names of those loved long ago,

exiled by Life. And like a statue's wide
gaze is hers. Serene and grave, her voice
has the tone of those dear voices that have died.

VII. A UNE FEMME

A vous ces vers, de par la grâce consolante
De vos grands yeux où rit et pleure un rêve doux,
De par votre âme, pure et toute bonne, à vous
Ces vers du fond de ma détresse violente.

C'est qu'hélas! le hideux cauchemar qui me hante
N'a pas de trêve et va furieux, fou, jaloux,
Se multipliant comme un cortège de loups
Et se pendant après mon sort qu'il ensanglante.

Oh! je souffre, je souffre affreusement, si bien
Que le gémissement premier du premier homme
Chassé d'Éden n'est qu'une églogue au prix du mien!

Et les soucis que vous pouvez avoir sont comme
Des hirondelles sur un ciel d'après-midi,
—Chère,—par un beau jour de septembre attiédi.

VII. TO A WOMAN

For the consoling grace, and as its due,
of your great eyes where a sweet dream laughs and weeps,
and for your pure, kind soul, out of my deep
and violent distress this verse for you.

Alas, the hideous nightmare without truce
haunts me and with furious, jealous speed,
increasing like a pack of wolves, pursues
and springs upon my fate and makes it bleed!

I suffer, suffer fiercely: the first groan
of the first man driven out of Eden
is an eclogue by contrast with my own!

And the small cares you have are like the play
of swallows, my dear, in the lovely heaven
of afternoon, on a warm September day.

EAUX-FORTES

❧

I. CROQUIS PARISIEN

La lune plaquait ses teintes de zinc
       Par angles obtus.
Des bouts de fumée en forme de cinq
Sortaient drus et noirs des hauts toits pointus.

Le ciel était gris, la bise pleurait
       Ainsi qu'un basson.
Au loin, un matou frileux et discret
Miaulait d'étrange et grêle façon.

Moi, j'allais, rêvant du divin Platon
       Et de Phidias,
Et de Salamine et de Marathon,
Sous l'œil clignotant des bleus becs de gaz.

ETCHINGS

❦

I. PARISIAN SKETCH

The moon was laying her plates of zinc
      on the oblique.
Like figure fives the plumes of smoke
rose thick and black from the tall roof-peaks.

In the gray sky the breeze wept loud
      as a bassoon.
In a funk a stealthy tomcat miaowed,
far away, his shrill strange tune.

Dreaming of Plato, I walked on,
      and of Phidias,
of Salamis and Marathon,
under winking eyes of blue jets of gas.

III. MARINE

L'Océan sonore
Palpite sous l'œil
De la lune en deuil
Et palpite encore,

Tandis qu'un éclair
Brutal et sinistre
Fend le ciel de bistre
D'un long zigzag clair,

Et que chaque lame,
En bonds convulsifs,
Le long des récifs,
Va, vient, luit et clame,

Et qu'au firmament,
Où l'ouragan erre,
Rugit le tonnerre
Formidablement.

III. MARINE

The sonorous ocean
throbs, under the eye
of the sad moon on high,
in palpitant motion,

while a white lightning-flash,
brutal and sinister,
cuts the sky's bister
with a long zigzag gash;

the waves, all the waves,
with convulsive strength
along the reef's length
go and come, shine and rave;

in the sky's empery,
where the hurricane wanders,
rumbles the thunder
formidably.

IV. EFFET DE NUIT

La nuit. La pluie. Un ciel blafard que déchiquette
De flèches et de tours à jour la silhouette
D'une ville gothique éteinte au lointain gris.
La plaine. Un gibet plein de pendus rabougris
Secoués par le bec avide des corneilles
Et dansant dans l'air noir des gigues nonpareilles,
Tandis que leurs pieds sont la pâture des loups.
Quelques buissons d'épine épars, et quelques houx
Dressant l'horreur de leur feuillage à droite, à gauche,
Sur le fuligineux fouillis d'un fond d'ébauche.
Et puis, autour de trois livides prisonniers
Qui vont pieds nus, deux cent vingt-cinq pertuisaniers
En marche, et leurs fers droits, comme des fers de herse,
Luisent à contresens des lances de l'averse.

IV. NIGHT EFFECT

Night. Rain. A lurid sky that lets
the spires and towers show gray silhouettes
of an old Gothic town by distance dimmed.
The plain. A gibbet where stiffs dwindle, trimmed
by greedy crows' beaks, dancing in black air
jigs unparalleled in any fair,
even while the wolves are pasturing on their toes.
Some scraggly thornbush; and the holly shows
its leafy horror, right and left, crosshatched
as on the murky background of a sketch.
Then, with three livid barefoot prisoners,
two hundred five and twenty halberdiers:
like harrow-teeth, pikes gleam against the grain
of the diagonal lances of the rain.

V. GROTESQUES

Leurs jambes pour toutes montures,
Pour tous biens l'or de leurs regards,
Par le chemin des aventures
Ils vont haillonneux et hagards.

Le sage, indigné, les harangue;
Le sot plaint ces fous hasardeux;
Les enfants leur tirent la langue
Et les filles se moquent d'eux.

C'est qu'odieux et ridicules,
Et maléfiques en effet,
Ils ont l'air, sur les crépuscules,
D'un mauvais rêve que l'on fait:

C'est que, sur leurs aigres guitares
Crispant la main des libertés,
Ils nasillent des chants bizarres,
Nostalgiques et révoltés;

C'est enfin que dans leurs prunelles
Rit et pleure—fastidieux—
L'amour des choses éternelles,
Des vieux morts et des anciens dieux!

(Continued on page 24)

V. GROTESQUES

Their legs for their only nags,
no wealth but the gold of their glance,
they go, untamed, in rags,
along the road of chance.

Sadly the fool condemns
these madmen; the sage harangues;
children stick out their tongues,
and the girls make fun of them.

Droll and malevolent
and odious, they seem,
with shades of twilight blent,
part of an evil dream;

they make thrill with licentious
hands their shrill guitars
and sing through the nose rebellious
songs, homesick and bizarre;

in their eyes, through smiles and tears,
wearily love lauds
eternal things, the years'
dead, and the ancient gods!

(Continued on page 25)

GROTESQUES—*Continued*

—Donc, allez, vagabonds sans trêves,
Errez, funestes et maudits,
Le long des gouffres et des grèves,
Sous l'œil fermé des paradis!

La nature à l'homme s'allie
Pour châtier comme il le faut
L'orgueilleuse mélancolie
Qui vous fait marcher le front haut.

Et, vengeant sur vous le blasphème
Des vastes espoirs véhéments,
Meurtrit votre front anathème
Au choc rude des éléments.

Les juins brûlent et les décembres
Gèlent votre chair jusqu'aux os,
Et la fièvre envahit vos membres,
Qui se déchirent aux roseaux.

Tout vous repousse et tout vous navre,
Et quand la mort viendra pour vous,
Maigre et froide, votre cadavre
Sera dédaigné par les loups!

GROTESQUES—*Continued*

—Dismal and doomed to wander,
vagabonds all despise,
by pits and shores, under
heaven's tight-closed eyes!

Nature and man are allied
to punish—and properly—
the melancholy pride
that walks with forehead high,

and, avenging the blasphemy
of your vast hope's vehemence,
they bruise your accursèd brows
with shocks of rude elements.

Junes burn and Decembers freeze
clean to the bone your flesh;
fever shakes your knees,
you could tear yourself on a rush.

You whom all things spurn
and wound, when death shall come,
even the wolves will scorn
your cadaver, starved and numb.

❧

V. CHANSON D'AUTOMNE

Les sanglots longs
Des violons
   De l'automne
Blessent mon cœur
D'une langueur
   Monotone.

Tout suffocant
Et blême, quand
   Sonne l'heure,
Je me souviens
Des jours anciens
   Et je pleure;

Et je m'en vais
Au vent mauvais
   Qui m'emporte
Deçà, delà,
Pareil à la
   Feuille morte.

Mournful Landscapes

❦

V. AUTUMN SONG

With long sobs
the violin-throbs
    of autumn wound
my heart with languorous
and monotonous
    sound.

Choking and pale
when I mind the tale
    the hours keep,
my memory strays
down other days
    and I weep;

and I let me go
where ill winds blow,
    now here, now there,
harried and sped,
even as a dead
    leaf, anywhere.

VI. L'HEURE DU BERGER

La lune est rouge au brumeux horizon;
Dans un brouillard qui danse, la prairie
S'endort fumeuse, et la grenouille crie
Par les joncs verts où circule un frisson;

Les fleurs des eaux referment leurs corolles,
Des peupliers profilent aux lointains,
Droits et serrés, leurs spectres incertains;
Vers les buissons errent les lucioles;

Les chats-huants s'éveillent, et sans bruit
Rament l'air noir avec leurs ailes lourdes,
Et le zénith s'emplit de lueurs sourdes.
Blanche, Vénus émerge, et c'est la Nuit.

VI. DUSK

The moon is red in the foggy sky;
in a dancing mist the meadow sleeps
under the reek, and the frogs cry
in the green reeds where a shudder creeps;

the water-lilies close their spathes,
the poplars profile far away,
straight and serried, their vague wraiths;
among the thickets fireflies stray;

the horned owls waken now and row
with heavy wings in silent flight,
the zenith fills with a dull glow.
Pale, Venus comes forth; and it is Night.

CAPRICES

I. FEMME ET CHATTE

Elle jouait avec sa chatte;
Et c'était merveille de voir
La main blanche et la blanche patte
S'ébattre dans l'ombre du soir.

Elle cachait—la scélérate!—
Sous ces mitaines de fil noir
Ses meurtriers ongles d'agate,
Coupants et clairs comme un rasoir.

L'autre aussi faisait la sucrée
Et rentrait sa griffe acérée,
Mais le diable n'y perdait rien...

Et dans le boudoir où, sonore,
Tintait son rire aérien,
Brillaient quatre points de phosphore.

CAPRICES

🎖

I. WOMAN AND CAT

She was playing with her cat,
and it was marvelous to see
white hand and white paw, pitty-pat,
spar in the evening sportively.

The little wretch hid in her paws,
those black silk mittens, murderously,
the deadly agate of her claws,
keen as a razor's edge can be.

Her steel drawn in, the other seemed
all sugar, the sly hypocrite,
but the devil didn't lose a bit . . .

and in the room where, sonorous,
her airy laughter rang, there gleamed
four sharp points of phosphorous.

III. LA CHANSON DES INGÉNUES

Nous sommes les Ingénues
Aux bandeaux plats, à l'œil bleu,
Qui vivons, presque inconnues,
Dans les romans qu'on lit peu.

Nous allons entrelacées,
Et le jour n'est pas plus pur
Que le fond de nos pensées,
Et nos rêves sont d'azur;

Et nous courons par les prés
Et rions et babillons
Des aubes jusqu'aux vesprées,
Et chassons aux papillons;

Et des chapeaux de bergères
Défendent notre fraîcheur,
Et nos robes—si légères—
Sont d'une extrême blancheur;

(Continued on page 34)

III. SONG OF THE INGENUES

Ingenues, not quite grown,
blue-eyed, braids round the head,
we live almost unknown
in novels not much read.

With our arms intertwined,
we walk; pure as sunbeams
is our subconscious mind,
and we have azure dreams;

laughing, we race through the meadows,
prattling, from sunrise
to the fall of evening shadows,
chasing the butterflies;

shepherdess bonnets quite
preserve our young fresh skin,
and our frocks—so thin—
are of immaculate white;

(Continued on page 35)

Les Richelieux, les Caussades
Et les chevaliers Faublas
Nous prodiguent les œillades,
Les saluts et les «hélas!»

Mais en vain, et leurs mimiques
Se viennent casser le nez
Devant les plis ironiques
De nos jupons détournés;

Et notre candeur se raille
Des imaginations
De ces raseurs de muraille,
Bien que parfois nous sentions

Battre nos cœurs sous nos mantes
A des pensers clandestins,
En nous sachant les amantes
Futures des libertins.

SONG OF THE INGENUES—*Continued*

the Richelieus and rakes make passes,
the cavaliers sheep's eyes,
all prodigal of sighs
and greetings and 'alases!'

in vain—they have no luck;
they get their noses hurt
on the ironic tucks
of the evasive skirt.

Ingenuously we rail
at the imaginations
of these climbers of the wall,
although the perturbations,

wild thumpings of our hearts,
inform our secret dreams
that we're the future tarts
of these same libertines.

SÉRÉNADE

Comme la voix d'un mort qui chanterait
            Du fond de sa fosse,
Maîtresse, entends monter vers ton retrait
            Ma voix aigre et fausse.

Ouvre ton âme et ton oreille au son
            De la mandoline:
Pour toi j'ai fait, pour toi, cette chanson
            Cruelle et câline.

Je chanterai tes yeux d'or et d'onyx
            Purs de toutes ombres,
Puis le Léthé de ton sein, puis le Styx
            De tes cheveux sombres.

Comme la voix d'un mort qui chanterait
            Du fond de sa fosse,
Maîtresse, entends monter vers ton retrait
            Ma voix aigre et fausse.

(Continued on page 38)

SERENADE

Even as the voice of one dead might sing
       from the depths of the vaults,
mistress, in your room you hear ring
       my voice shrill and false.

Open your ears to my mandolin's sound
       and open your soul:
for you I made it, for you, this song,
       to hurt and cajole.

I will sing your eyes of onyx and gold,
       of shadows pure,
then the Lethe of your breast, then the cold
       Styx of your hair.

Even as the voice of one dead might sing
       from the depths of the vaults,
mistress, in your room you hear ring
       my voice shrill and false.

(Continued on page 39)

37

SÉRÉNADE—*Continued*

Puis je louerai beaucoup, comme il convient,
    Cette chair bénie
Dont le parfum opulent me revient
    Les nuits d'insomnie.

Et pour finir, je dirai le baiser
    De ta lèvre rouge,
Et ta douceur à me martyriser,
    —Mon Ange!—ma Gouge!

Ouvre ton âme et ton oreille au son
    De ma mandoline:
Pour toi j'ai fait, pour toi, cette chanson
    Cruelle et câline.

SERENADE—*Continued*

Then I will praise much, as is right,
       this blessed flesh
whose rich perfume haunts many a night
       of sleeplessness.

And to conclude, I'll sing the kiss
       of your red lips which
with your sweetness martyrize me in bliss,
       —my Angel!—my gouging Bitch!

Open your ears to my mandolin's sound
       and open your soul:
for you I made it, for you, this song,
       to hurt and cajole.

NOCTURNE PARISIEN

Roule, roule ton flot indolent, morne Seine,—
Sous tes ponts qu'environne une vapeur malsaine
Bien des corps ont passé, morts, horribles, pourris,
Dont les âmes avaient pour meurtrier Paris.
Mais tu n'en traînes pas, en tes ondes glacées,
Autant que ton aspect m'inspire de pensées!

Le Tibre a sur ses bords des ruines qui font
Monter le voyageur vers un passé profond,
Et qui, de lierre noir et de lichen couvertes,
Apparaissent, tas gris, parmi les herbes vertes.
Le gai Guadalquivir rit aux blonds orangers
Et reflète, les soirs, des boléros légers,
Le Pactole a son or, le Bosphore a sa rive
Où vient faire son kief l'odalisque lascive.
Le Rhin est un burgrave, et c'est un troubadour
Que le Lignon, et c'est un ruffian que l'Adour.
Le Nil, au bruit plaintif de ses eaux endormies,
Berce de rêves doux le sommeil des momies.
Le grand Meschascébé, fier de ses joncs sacrés,
Charrie augustement ses îlots mordorés,
Et soudain, beau d'éclairs, de fracas et de fastes,
Splendidement s'écroule en Niagaras vastes.
L'Eurotas, où l'essaim des cygnes familiers
Mêle sa grâce blanche au vert mat des lauriers,
Sous son ciel clair que raie un vol de gypaète,
Rhythmique et caressant, chante ainsi qu'un poète.
Enfin, Ganga, parmi les hauts palmiers tremblants
Et les rouges padmas, marche à pas fiers et lents

(Continued on page 42)

PARISIAN NOCTURNE

Roll, gloomy Seine, roll down your indolent flood,—
under your bridges where sickly vapors brood
how many a body's passed, dead, bloated, foul,
and it is Paris that has killed the soul.
But nothing drifts along your icy stream
so powerful as your face to make me dream!

Along the Tiber's banks old ruins massed
make travelers climb toward a mighty past;
in the green grass, gray rubble-heaps, they shine
among the lichen and black ivy vine.
On gay Guadalquivir at night one sees
boleros danced in mirrored orange-trees.
Lewd odalisques beside the Bosphorus
come to smoke hemp. There's gold in Pactolus.
The Rhine's a burgrave, and a troubadour
is the Lignon, a brawler the Adour.
The Nile with plaintive murmurs from the deep
cradles in soft dreams the mummies' sleep.
Great Mississippi, proud of its sacred rushes,
bears grandly floating isles of red-brown bushes,
and swiftly bursts, with pomp of roaring spray,
in lovely lightnings, like Niagara's play.
Eurotas, where white swans in friendly swarms
with the dull green of laurel blend their charms,
below clear skies that shine with griffons' wings,
rhythmic, caressing, sings as a poet sings.
And finally, Ganges, regally clad, below
red padmas and tall trembling palms, with slow

(Continued on page 43)

En appareil royal, tandis qu'au loin la foule
Le long des temples va, hurlant, vivante houle,
Au claquement massif des cymbales de bois,
Et qu'accroupi, filant ses notes de hautbois,
De saut de l'antilope agile attendant l'heure,
Le tigre jaune au dos rayé s'étire et pleure.

—Toi, Seine, tu n'as rien. Deux quais, et voilà tout,
Deux quais crasseux, semés de l'un à l'autre bout
D'affreux bouquins moisis et d'une foule insigne
Qui fait dans l'eau des ronds et qui pêche à la ligne.
Oui, mais quand vient le soir, raréfiant enfin
Les passants alourdis de sommeil ou de faim,
Et que le couchant met au ciel des taches rouges
Qu'il fait bon aux rêveurs descendre de leurs bouges
Et, s'accoudant au pont de la Cité, devant
Notre-Dame, songer cœur et cheveux au vent!
Les nuages, chassés par la brise nocturne,
Courent, cuivreux et roux, dans l'azur taciturne.
Sur la tête d'un roi du portail, le soleil,
Au moment de mourir, pose un baiser vermeil.
L'Hirondelle s'enfuit à l'approche de l'ombre.
Et l'on voit voleter la chauve-souris sombre.
Tout bruit s'apaise autour. A peine un vague son
Dit que la ville est là qui chante sa chanson,
Qui lèche ses tyrans et qui mord ses victimes;
Et c'est l'aube des vols, des amours et des crimes.
—Puis, tout à coup, ainsi qu'un ténor effaré
Lançant dans l'air bruni son cri désespéré,

(Continued on page 44)

proud steps moves on, while far away crowds rave
before the temple, like a living wave,
to the thunderous clacking of the wooden cymbals;
while, crouched and purring with deep oboe-rumbles,
waiting until the nimble antelope leaps,
the tawny stripèd tiger lolls and weeps.

—You, Seine, have nothing. Two quays, and that's all,
two dirty quays with musty old bookstalls
littered from end to end, and a low crowd
make rings in the water, fishing with line and rod.
Yes, but when evening has thinned out the loungers,
stupified with drowsiness and hunger,
and sunset reddens the sky with freckles, then
how it fetches the dreamers forth from lair and den,
to lean on the Pont de la Cité and dream,
heart and hair to the wind, near Notre-Dame!
Pursued by the night breeze, the cloud-banks fly,
copper-red, through the silent azure sky.
Pressing a rosy kiss on the king's brow
by the west door, the dying sun sinks low.
The swallow flees the shadows of the night,
and here the bat comes, staggering in her flight.
The noise dies down. Vaguely before long
one hears the city hum its evening song,
that fawns on its tyrants and gnaws its sufferers;
this is the dawn of crimes, thefts, and amours.
—Then, all at once, a tenor with wild eyes
hurls on the darkened air his desperate cries,

(Continued on page 45)

Son cri qui se lamente, et se prolonge, et crie,
Éclate en quelque coin l'orgue de Barbarie:
Il brame un de ces airs, romances ou polkas,
Qu'enfants nous tapotions sur nos harmonicas
Et qui font, lents ou vifs, réjouissants ou tristes,
Vibrer l'âme aux proscrits, aux femmes, aux artistes.
C'est écorché, c'est faux, c'est horrible, c'est dur,
Et donnerait la fièvre à Rossini, pour sûr;
Ces rires sont traînés, ces plaintes sont hachées;
Sur une clef de *sol* impossible juchées,
Les notes ont un rhume et les *do* sont des *la,*
Mais qu'importe! l'on pleure en entendant cela!
Mais l'esprit, transporté dans le pays des rêves,
Sent à ces vieux accords couler en lui des sèves;
La pitié monte au cœur et les larmes aux yeux,
Et l'on voudrait pouvoir goûter la paix des cieux,
Et dans une harmonie étrange et fantastique
Qui tient de la musique et tient de la plastique,
L'âme, les inondant de lumière et de chant,
Mêle les sons de l'orgue aux rayons du couchant!

—Et puis l'orgue s'éloigne, et puis c'est le silence,
Et la nuit terne arrive et Vénus se balance
Sur une molle nue au fond des cieux obscurs:
On allume les becs de gaz le long des murs.
Et l'astre et les flambeaux font des zigzags fantasques
Dans le fleuve plus noir que le velours des masques;
Et le contemplateur sur le haut garde-fou
Par l'air et par les ans rouillé comme un vieux sou

(Concluded on page 46)

with long-drawn-out laments; that noisy mourner
the barrel-organ bursts forth on the corner,
groaning a ballad, polka, or some tune
that children hammer from our xylophones,
and fast or slow, mournful or gay, whatever,
makes the souls of outcasts, women, and artists quiver.
Such music, murdered, horrible, false, impure,
would give Rossini fever-chills, for sure;
those laughs are dragged out, the laments are chopped;
the notes on one impossible *sol* are stopped
and have a head-cold; all the *do*'s are *la*'s,
but what's the difference! We weep because
those old chords bear the soul to lands of dreams
and through our bodies all the strong sap teems;
pity wells in the heart, tears in the eyes,
and one wants to taste the quiet of the skies;
in harmonies outlandish and fantastic
that draw from arts, both musical and plastic,
the soul, flooding them with light and song,
mingles the organ-tones with the setting sun!

—The organ moves on. Tarnished night sinks over
the silence of the town, and Venus hovers
on a soft cloud in her dark retreat;
gas-jets are lighted all along the street;
on the river, blacker than velvet masks,
the stars and lamps make zigzags and arabesques;
on the high rail, corroded like old sous
by the air and the years, one leans to muse,

(Concluded on page 47)

Se penche, en proie aux vents néfastes de l'abîme.
Pensée, espoir serein, ambition sublime,
Tout, jusqu'au souvenir, tout s'envole, tout fuit,
Et l'on est seul avec Paris, l'Onde et la Nuit!

—Sinistre trinité! De l'ombre dures portes!
Mané-Thécel-Pharès des illusions mortes!
Vous êtes toutes trois, ô Goules de malheur,
Si terribles, que l'Homme, ivre de la douleur
Que lui font en perçant sa chair vos doigts de spectre,
L'Homme, espèce d'Oreste à qui manque une Électre,
Sous la fatalité de votre regard creux
Ne peut rien et va droit au précipice affreux;
Et vous êtes aussi toutes trois si jalouses
De tuer et d'offrir au grand Ver des épouses
Qu'on ne sait que choisir entre vos trois horreurs,
Et si l'on craindrait moins périr par les terreurs
Des Ténèbres que sous l'Eau sourde, l'Eau profonde,
Ou dans tes bras fardés, Paris, reine du monde!

—Et tu coules toujours, Seine, et, tout en rampant,
Tu traînes dans Paris ton cours de vieux serpent,
De vieux serpent boueux, emportant vers tes havres
Tes cargaisons de bois, de houille et de cadavres!

PARISIAN NOCTURNE—*Concluded*

a prey to the abyss's ominous wind.
Calm hope, sublime ambition, the thoughtful mind,
all, even memory, on swift wings takes flight,
and one is alone with Paris, the Flood, and Night!

—Sinister trinity! Cruel gates of shade!
Mene, tekel, upharsin of illusions dead!
You are all three, O dark Ghouls of misfortune,
so terrible that Man, drunk of affliction,
whose flesh you tear, you bony-fingered specters,
Man, a kind of Orestes lacking Electra,
feels the fatality of your hollow gaze
and can do nothing but plunge into space;
you are, all three of you, also so zealous
to kill and offer the Great Worm bedfellows,
that one can only choose among three horrors,
if he'd fear less to perish by the terrors
of Gloom, or be in perilous Waters swirled,
or in your rouged arms, Paris, queen of the world!

—And you run on forever, Seine, all rampant,
drawing through Paris your trail of the old serpent,
muddy old serpent, bearing to your harbors
cargoes of coal and lumber and cadavers!

CÉSAR BORGIA

PORTRAIT EN PIED

Sur fond sombre noyant un riche vestibule
Où le buste d'Horace et celui de Tibulle
Lointain et de profil rêvent en marbre blanc,
La main gauche au poignard et la main droite au flanc,
Tandis qu'un rire doux redresse la moustache,
Le duc CÉSAR, en grand costume, se détache.
Les yeux noirs, les cheveux noirs et le velours noir
Vont contrastant, parmi l'or somptueux d'un soir,
Avec la pâleur mate et belle du visage
Vu de trois quarts et très ombré, suivant l'usage
Des Espagnols ainsi que des Vénitiens,
Dans les portraits de rois et de patriciens.
Le nez palpite, fin et droit. La bouche, rouge,
Est mince, et l'on dirait que la tenture bouge
Au souffle véhément qui doit s'en exhaler.
Et le regard errant avec laisser-aller,
Devant lui, comme il sied aux anciennes peintures,
Fourmille de pensers énormes d'aventures.
Et le front, large et pur, sillonné d'un grand pli,
Sans doute de projets formidables rempli,
Médite sous la toque où frissonne une plume
S'élançant hors d'un nœud de rubis qui s'allume.

CAESAR BORGIA

FULL-LENGTH PORTRAIT

Against the somber depths of a vestibule
in which the busts of Horace and Tibullus
are profiled in white marble as they dream,
Duke Caesar advances in his grand costume:
left hand on his poniard, right on hip,
with a soft smile lifting the thin lip
with the mustache. Black velvet, the black hair
and eyes, contrast, in evening's golden air,
with the dead pallid beauty of the face
seen at three-quarters, shadowed, as was the use
of painters, both the Spaniards and Venetians,
when they portrayed their monarchs and patricians.
Delicate and straight, the nostrils quiver.
The thin red mouth would make the curtains shiver
if ever he really breathed with vehemence.
And his glance, wandering with negligence
before him, as befits these ancient pictures,
swarms with enormous visions of adventures.
The broad clear brow, with deep-creased furrow, teems
undoubtedly with formidable schemes,
broods under a toque on which a shuddering plume
is clasped by rubies sparkling in the gloom.

FÊTES GALANTES

1869

CLAIR DE LUNE

Votre âme est un paysage choisi
Que vont charmants masques et bergamasques,
Jouant du luth et dansant et quasi
Tristes sous leurs déguisements fantasques.

Tout en chantant sur le mode mineur
L'amour vainqueur et la vie opportune,
Ils n'ont pas l'air de croire à leur bonheur
Et leur chanson se mêle au clair de lune,

Au calme clair de lune triste et beau,
Qui fait rêver les oiseaux dans les arbres
Et sangloter d'extase les jets d'eau,
Les grands jets d'eau sveltes parmi les marbres.

MOONLIGHT

Your soul is like a painter's landscape where
charming masks in shepherd mummeries
are playing lutes and dancing with an air
of being sad in their fantastic guise.

Even while they sing, all in a minor key,
of love triumphant and life's careless boon,
they seem in doubt of their felicity,
their song melts in the calm light of the moon,

the lovely melancholy light that sets
the little birds to dreaming in the tree
and among the statues makes the jets
of slender fountains sob with ecstasy.

PANTOMIME

Pierrot, qui n'a rien d'un Clitandre,
Vide un flacon sans plus attendre,
Et, pratique, entame un pâté.

Cassandre, au fond de l'avenue,
Verse une larme méconnue
Sur son neveu déshérité.

Ce faquin d'Arlequin combine
L'enlèvement de Colombine
Et pirouette quatre fois.

Colombine rêve, surprise
De sentir un cœur dans la brise
Et d'entendre en son cœur des voix.

PANTOMIME

Pierrot, no polite Clitandre,
in the flask leaves no remainder,
and, practical fellow, cuts a pie.

Cassandre down the avenue,
having cast off his nephew,
sheds a teardrop on the sly.

That scoundrel Harlequin designs
the kidnapping of Columbine
and makes four pirouettes with art.

Columbine dreams, surprised to find
she feels a heart along the wind
and hears strange voices in her heart.

SUR L'HERBE

L'abbé divague.—Et toi, marquis,
Tu mets de travers ta perruque.
—Ce vieux vin de Chypre est exquis
Moins, Camargo, que votre nuque.

—Ma flamme . . . —Do, mi, sol, la, si.
—L'abbé, ta noirceur se dévoile.
—Que je meure, Mesdames, si
Je ne vous décroche une étoile.

—Je voudrais être petit chien!
—Embrassons nos bergères, l'une
Après l'autre.—Messieurs, eh bien?
—Do, mi, sol.—Hé! bonsoir la Lune!

ON THE GRASS

The abbé's raving.—You, marquis,
have put on crosswise your peruke.
—Old Cyprus wine's no charm for me,
compared, Camargo, with your neck.

—My flame . . . —Do, mi, sol, la, si.
—Abbé, your villainy's laid bare!
—May I die, ladies, instantly,
if I don't unhook for you a star.

—A lapdog's life's the life for me!
—Let's kiss our shepherdesses soon,
one after t'other.—You agree?
—Do, mi, sol.—Hey! Good evening, Moon!

L'ALLÉE

Fardée et peinte comme au temps des bergeries,
Frêle parmi les nœuds énormes de rubans,
Elle passe, sous les ramures assombries,
Dans l'allée où verdit la mousse des vieux bancs,
Avec mille façons et mille afféteries
Qu'on garde d'ordinaire aux perruches chéries.
Sa longue robe à queue est bleue, et l'éventail
Qu'elle froisse en ses doigts fluets aux larges bagues
S'égaie en des sujets érotiques, si vagues
Qu'elle sourit, tout en rêvant, à maint détail.
—Blonde en somme. Le nez mignon avec la bouche
Incarnadine, grasse, et divine d'orgueil
Inconscient.—D'ailleurs plus fine que la mouche
Qui ravive l'éclat un peu niais de l'œil.

THE GARDEN PATH

Painted and rouged as in mock-pastoral days,
frail among the enormous furbelows,
she passes, underneath the somber branches,
along the walk with ancient moss-grown benches;
the thousand coquetries that she displays
are such as any pampered parrot knows.
Her long-trained robe is blue. Her fan unveils
and hides, in her slim hands with heavy rings,
such vaguely painted gay erotic things
that she smiles, dreaming, over the details.
—In short, a blonde. The darling nose, full mouth,
carnation, goddess-like with pride. Likewise,
more subtle even than the artful mouche
which points the brilliant, somewhat foolish, eyes.

LES INGÉNUS

Les hauts talons luttaient avec les longues jupes,
En sorte que, selon le terrain et le vent,
Parfois luisaient des bas de jambe, trop souvent
Interceptés!—et nous aimions ce jeu de dupes.

Parfois aussi le dard d'un insecte jaloux
Inquiétait le col des belles, sous les branches,
Et c'était des éclairs soudains de nuques blanches
Et ce régal comblait nos jeunes yeux de fous.

Le soir tombait, un soir équivoque d'automne:
Les belles, se pendant rêveuses à nos bras,
Dirent alors des mots si spécieux, tout bas,
Que notre âme depuis ce temps tremble et s'étonne.

THE UNSOPHISTICATES

The high heels fighting with the trailing skirts
on the uneven ground, at the wind's whim,
showed often a swift flash of shining limb,
soon intercepted!—how we loved the sport!

Sometimes the stings of greedy bugs and flies
under the branches bothered pretty necks;
then there were intimate white lightning-peeks,
a feast that overwhelmed young foolish eyes.

Evening, the autumn twilight that dissembles,
evening fell, and the lovely dreamers leaning
on our arms murmured words whose specious meaning
since then has set our startled souls atremble.

CORTÈGE

Un singe en veste de brocart
Trotte et gambade devant elle
Qui froisse un mouchoir de dentelle
Dans sa main gantée avec art,

Tandis qu'un négrillon tout rouge
Maintient à tour de bras les pans
De sa lourde robe en suspens,
Attentif à tout pli qui bouge;

Le singe ne perd pas des yeux
La gorge blanche de la dame.
Opulent trésor que réclame
Le torse nu de l'un des dieux;

Le négrillon parfois soulève
Plus haut qu'il ne faut, l'aigrefin,
Son fardeau somptueux, afin
De voir ce dont la nuit il rêve;

Elle va par les escaliers,
Et ne paraît pas davantage
Sensible à l'insolent suffrage
De ses animaux familiers.

RETINUE

A playful monkey frisks with grand
gambols, in brocaded vest,
in front of her who idly twists
her kerchief in a well-gloved hand.

A red-garbed little negro holds
at his arms' length the heavy train
of her robe and takes some pains
to keep in order all the folds.

Never does the monkey nod
or from those white breasts drop his eyes;
those lovely riches were a prize
for the naked body of a god.

The negro lad, sharp little wight,
sometimes lifts a bit too high
the sumptuous burden, so his eye
can see what he dreams of at night.

She goes upstairs, ignoring all,
pretending to be unaware
of the insolent approving stare
of her familiar animals.

LES COQUILLAGES

Chaque coquillage incrusté
Dans la grotte où nous nous aimâmes
A sa particularité.

L'un a la pourpre de nos âmes
Dérobée au sang de nos cœurs
Quand je brûle et que tu t'enflammes;

Cet autre affecte tes langueurs
Et tes pâleurs alors que, lasse,
Tu m'en veux de mes yeux moqueurs;

Celui-ci contrefait la grâce
De ton oreille, et celui-là
Ta nuque rose, courte et grasse;

Mais un, entre autres, me troubla.

THE SHELLS

In the grotto by the sea
where we loved, each crusted shell
has its singularity.

This, purple as our souls' desire,
as blood stolen from our hearts
when I burn and you catch fire;

this affects your pallid languor
when you have tired, and mockery
in my eyes has stirred your anger;

this one counterfeits the shape
of your ear; in this I see
your neck's chubby rosy nape;

but one, among them, troubled me.

FANTOCHES

Scaramouche et Pulcinella,
Qu'un mauvais dessein rassembla,
Gesticulent, noirs sur la lune.

Cependant l'excellent docteur
Bolonais cueille avec lenteur
Des simples parmi l'herbe brune.

Lors sa fille, piquant minois,
Sous la charmille en tapinois
Se glisse demi-nue, en quête

De son beau pirate espagnol,
Dont un langoureux rossignol
Clame la détresse à tue-tête.

PUPPETS

Scaramouche has come to plot
with Pulcinella: a bad lot,
they make black shadows on the moon.

The doctor from Bologna picks
herbs to medicine the sick
in the grasses sere and brown.

But his daughter with piquant eye
to the arbor, on the sly,
glides half-naked on a quest

for her fine buccaneer of Spain,
whose anguish cries in the loud pain
the nightingale pours from his breast.

CYTHÈRE

Un pavillon à claires-voies
Abrite doucement nos joies
Qu'éventent des rosiers amis;

L'odeur des roses, faible, grâce
Au vent léger d'été qui passe,
Se mêle aux parfums qu'elle a mis;

Comme ses yeux l'avaient promis,
Son courage est grand et sa lèvre
Communique une exquise fièvre;

Et l'Amour comblant tout, hormis
La Faim, sorbets et confitures
Nous préservent des courbatures.

CYTHERA

The latticed arbor tenderly
hides our joys which the rose tree
fans and cools with pleasant air;

the languid fragrance of the rose,
thanks to the summer breeze that blows,
blends with the perfume that she wears;

her eyes' promise has been kept:
she is fearless and the favors
of her lips are exquisite fevers;

Love having sated all, except
Hunger—sherbets and preserves
keep intact our bodies' curves.

EN BATEAU

L'étoile du berger tremblote
Dans l'eau plus noire et le pilote
Cherche un briquet dans sa culotte.

C'est l'instant, Messieurs, ou jamais,
D'être audacieux, et je mets
Mes deux mains partout désormais!

Le chevalier Atys qui gratte
Sa guitare, à Chloris l'ingrate
Lance une œillade scélérate.

L'abbé confesse bas Églé,
Et ce vicomte déréglé
Des champs donne à son cœur la clé.

Cependant la lune se lève
Et l'esquif en sa course brève
File gaîment sur l'eau qui rêve.

BOATING

Venus trembles over beaches
and black waves; the pilot searches
for the tinder in his breeches.

Gentlemen, it's now or never
to make a pass—and I maneuver
both hands, any goal whatever!

Courtly Atys, making cry
his guitar, gives on the sly
faithless Chloris a mean eye.

The abbé has confessed Eglé,
and the viscount, all too gay,
lets his heart make holiday.

Meanwhile comes the moon and beams
as the sailboat gaily skims
briefly over waves of dreams.

LE FAUNE

Un vieux faune de terre cuite
Rit au centre des boulingrins,
Présageant sans doute une suite
Mauvaise à ces instants sereins

Qui m'ont conduit et t'ont conduite,
Mélancoliques pèlerins,
Jusqu'à cette heure dont la fuite
Tournoie au son des tambourins.

THE FAUN

A terra-cotta faun, quite old,
is laughing on the bowling-green;
doubtless a wretched end's foretold
for these bright moments and serene

which have led me and led you here—
and mournful pilgrims we have been!—
to this hour which now disappears,
twirled by the tinkling tambourine.

A CLYMÈNE

Mystiques barcarolles,
Romances sans paroles,
Chère, puisque tes yeux,
    Couleur des cieux,

Puisque ta voix, étrange
Vision qui dérange
Et trouble l'horizon
    De ma raison,

Puisque l'arome insigne
De ta pâleur de cygne
Et puisque la candeur
    De ton odeur,

Ah! puisque tout ton être,
Musique qui pénètre,
Nimbes d'anges défunts,
    Tons et parfums,

A sur d'almes cadences
En ses correspondances,
Induit mon cœur subtil,
    Ainsi soit-il!

TO CLYMÈNE

Romances without words,
mystic barcaroles heard,
dear, because your eyes,
    color of skies,

because your voice, strange
visions which derange
and trouble the horizon
    of my reason,

because the noble perfume
of your pallor's swan-plume
and because of the candor
    of your odor,

ah, because all your person—
music imbuing, piercing;
voice, perfume, the nimbs
    of dead seraphim—

has, with soft cadences
in its correspondences,
lured my heart's subtlety,
    so let it be!

LES INDOLENTS

Bah! malgré les destins jaloux,
Mourons ensemble, voulez-vous?
—La proposition est rare.

—Le rare est le bon. Donc mourons
Comme dans les Décamérons.
—Hi! hi! hi! quel amant bizarre!

—Bizarre, je ne sais. Amant
Irréprochable, assurément.
Si vous voulez, mourons ensemble?

—Monsieur, vous raillez mieux encor
Que vous n'aimez, et parlez d'or;
Mais taisons-nous, si bon vous semble?

Si bien que ce soir-là Tircis
Et Dorimène, à deux assis
Non loin de deux silvains hilares,

Eurent l'inexpiable tort
D'ajourner une exquise mort.
Hi! hi! hi! les amants bizarres!

THE INDOLENT ONES

Bah, despite jealous destinies,
let's die together, if you please!
—Well, your proposition's rare.

—What's rare is good. Let's die—come on—
as they did in the *Decameron*.
—Ha! ha! as a lover you're bizarre!

—Bizarre? I don't know. But as lover,
faultless surely. Think it over.
Let's die together, if you will.

—You're a better joker, sir, than lover,
you make fine talk; but wouldn't you rather
we'd just sit here and keep still?

Hence tonight it happened that
Dorimène and Tircis sat
not far from a boisterous sylvan pair

and irremissibly did wrong,
postponing an exquisite death too long.
Ha! ha! these lovers! How bizarre!

COLOMBINE

Léandre le sot,
Pierrot qui d'un saut
De puce
Franchit le buisson,
Cassandre sous son
Capuce,

Arlequin aussi,
Cet aigrefin si
Fantasque
Aux costumes fous,
Ses yeux luisants sous
Son masque,

—Do, mi, sol, mi, fa,—
Tout ce monde va,
Rit, chante
Et danse devant
Une belle enfant
Méchante

(Continued on page 80)

COLUMBINE

Leandre is simple,
Pierrot with nimble
    flea-hop
leaps the brushwood,
Cassandre with hood
    on his top,

Harlequin, droll
wag but no fool
    and brisk,
is dressed for the show—
and his eyes glow
    through his mask.

Do, mi, sol, do!
See everyone go
    with a laugh and a ditty;
dancing they whirl
before a bad girl
    but pretty,

(Continued on page 81)

Dont les yeux pervers
Comme les yeux verts
    Des chattes
Gardent ses appas
Et disent: «A bas
    Les pattes!»

—Eux ils vont toujours!
Fatidique cours
    Des astres,
Oh! dis-moi vers quels
Mornes ou cruels
    Désastres

L'implacable enfant,
Preste et relevant
    Ses jupes,
La rose au chapeau,
Conduit son troupeau
    De dupes?

whose eyes, green
as a cat's and obscene
    (she has cause
to guard her full-blown
charms), cry: "Keep down
    your paws!"

—Forever they go!
Stars who foreknow,
    say, to what
dismally dull
and pitiful
    lot

this implacable flirt,
lifting her skirt,
    rose in hair,
misleads her troupes,
poor gulls and dupes,
    where?

L'AMOUR PAR TERRE

Le vent de l'autre nuit a jeté bas l'Amour
Qui, dans le coin le plus mystérieux du parc,
Souriait en bandant malignement son arc,
Et dont l'aspect nous fit tant songer tout un jour!

Le vent de l'autre nuit l'a jeté bas! Le marbre
Au souffle du matin tournoie, épars. C'est triste
De voir le piédestal, où le nom de l'artiste
Se lit péniblement parmi l'ombre d'un arbre.

Oh! c'est triste de voir debout le piédestal
Tout seul! et des pensers mélancoliques vont
Et viennent dans mon rêve où le chagrin profond
Évoque un avenir solitaire et fatal.

Oh! c'est triste!—Et toi-même, est-ce pas? es touchée
D'un si dolent tableau, bien que ton œil frivole
S'amuse au papillon de pourpre et d'or qui vole
Au-dessus des débris dont l'allée est jonchée.

CUPID FALLEN

The wind blew little Cupid down last night,
who, in the dim nook of the park, with guile
bending his bow, would watch us with a smile,
and give us a long day of dream-delight.

Last night's wind blew him down. Ah! sad to see
the broken marble at the breath of dawn,
scattered, the artist's faint-seen name upon
the base, among the shadows of a tree.

Oh, it is sad, this empty base of stone,
and melancholy fancies enter in
and wander through my dream where deep chagrin
calls up a future fated and alone.

Oh, sad!—And you yourself, yes? feel the pain
of this drear picture, though your frivolous eye
toys with the gold-and-crimson butterfly
fluttering above the fragments in the lane.

EN SOURDINE

Calmes dans le demi-jour
Que les branches hautes font,
Pénétrons bien notre amour
De ce silence profond.

Fondons nos âmes, nos cœurs
Et nos sens extasiés,
Parmi les vagues langueurs
Des pins et des arbousiers.

Ferme tes yeux à demi,
Croise tes bras sur ton sein,
Et de ton cœur endormi
Chasse à jamais tout dessein.

Laissons-nous persuader
Au souffle berceur et doux
Qui vient à tes pieds rider
Les ondes de gazon roux.

Et quand, solennel, le soir
Des chênes noirs tombera,
Voix de notre désespoir,
Le rossignol chantera.

MUTED

Calmly in the twilight made
by the lofty boughs above,
let the silence here pervade
with profundity our love.

Let us join our souls, our senses,
and our hearts in ecstasies
among the uncertain languishments
of the pines and strawberry-trees.

Cross your arms upon your breast;
with your eyes half-closed, let dreams
from your heart that sinks to rest
chase forever all its schemes.

Let's convince ourselves, as sweet
and lulling little breezes pass,
making ripple at your feet
the russet billows of the grass.

And when from the dark oaks falls
solemn evening down the air,
then will sing the nightingales,
like the voice of our despair.

COLLOQUE SENTIMENTAL

Dans le vieux parc solitaire et glacé
Deux formes ont tout à l'heure passé.

Leurs yeux sont morts et leurs lèvres sont molles,
Et l'on entend à peine leurs paroles.

Dans le vieux parc solitaire et glacé
Deux spectres ont évoqué le passé.

—Te souvient-il de notre extase ancienne?
—Pourquoi voulez-vous donc qu'il m'en souvienne?

—Ton cœur bat-il toujours à mon seul nom?
Toujours vois-tu mon âme en rêve?—Non.

—Ah! les beaux jours de bonheur indicible
Où nous joignions nos bouches!—C'est possible.

Qu'il était bleu, le ciel, et grand l'espoir!
—L'espoir a fui, vaincu, vers le ciel noir.

Tels ils marchaient dans les avoines folles,
Et la nuit seule entendit leurs paroles.

SENTIMENTAL CONVERSATION

In the old solitary frozen park
two forms just passed and vanished in the dark.

Their lips were soft and slack, their eyes were dead,
and one could scarcely hear the words they said.

In the old lonely park nipped by the frost,
two specters have called back the past they lost.

—Do you remember our old ecstasies?
—Why would you have me waken those memories?

—When you hear my name does your heart always glow?
Do you always see my soul in dreams?—No.

—Ah, the good days of joy unspeakable
when our lips mingled!—That is possible.

—How blue the sky was then, and hope beat high!
—But hope fled, vanquished, down the gloomy sky.

Even so they walked through the wild oats, these dead,
and only the night heard the words they said.

LA BONNE CHANSON

✳ 1870 ✳

III

En robe grise et verte avec des ruches,
Un jour de juin que j'étais soucieux,
Elle apparut souriante à mes yeux
Qui l'admiraient sans redouter d'embûches.

Elle alla, vint, revint, s'assit, parla,
Légère et grave, ironique, attendrie:
Et je sentais en mon âme assombrie
Comme un joyeux reflet de tout cela;

Sa voix, étant de la musique fine,
Accompagnait délicieusement
L'esprit sans fiel de son babil charmant
Où la gaîté d'un cœur bon se devine.

Aussi soudain fus-je, après le semblant
D'une révolte aussitôt étouffée,
Au plein pouvoir de la petite Fée
Que depuis lors je supplie en tremblant.

III

In her dress of green and gray, with ruches,
one June day I was sick with care,
suddenly she was smiling there,
and I admired, nor feared ambushes.

She came and went, returned and sat
talking, ironic, tender, light,
and I felt my gloomy soul grow bright
with a gay reflection of all that;

deliciously her voice's tone
made a sweet music to her gentle
spirit's artless charming prattle
in which the kindly heart was shown.

Soon was I, my short dissembling
insurrection quickly quelled,
by the little Fairy's power enspelled,
whom since I've supplicated, trembling.

V

Avant que tu ne t'en ailles,
Pâle étoile du matin,
      —Mille cailles
Chantent, chantent dans le thym.—

Tourne devers le poète,
Dont les yeux sont pleins d'amour,
      —L'alouette
Monte au ciel avec le jour.—

Tourne ton regard que noie
L'aurore dans son azur;
      —Quelle joie
Parmi les champs de blé mûr!—

Puis fais luire ma pensée
Là-bas,—bien loin, oh! bien loin!
      —La rosée
Gaîment brille sur le foin.—

Dans le doux rêve où s'agite
Ma mie endormie encor...
      —Vite, vite,
Car voici le soleil d'or.—

V

Before you vanish, pale
star of morning prime
    (A thousand quail
are twittering in the thyme),

turn toward the poet's eyes
that are filled with love alway
    (Up the skies
the lark climbs with the day),

turn your gaze which drowns
in the auroral azure
    (Among the brown
ripe wheatfields, what pleasure!);

make my thoughts shine anew
down there, far, far away
    (The dew
shines cheerfully on the hay),

in the sweet dreams that prick
my dear still-sleepy one . . .
    (Quick! quick!
for here's the golden sun.)

VI

La lune blanche
Luit dans les bois;
De chaque branche
Part une voix
Sous la ramée...

O bien-aimée.

L'étang reflète,
Profond miroir,
La silhouette
Du saule noir
Où le vent pleure...

Rêvons, c'est l'heure.

Un vaste et tendre
Apaisement
Semble descendre
Du firmament
Que l'astre irise...

C'est l'heure exquise.

VI

The white moonglow
shines on the trees;
from each bough
a voice flees
as the leaves move . . .

Oh, my love.

The pond reflects,
a mirror deep,
the black silhouette
of the willow tree
where the wind weeps . . .

Oh, reverie.

Now a tender
and vast appeasement
seems to descend
from the firmament
with the irised star . . .

Ah, exquisite hour.

XIV

Le foyer, la lueur étroite de la lampe;
La rêverie avec le doigt contre la tempe
Et les yeux se perdant parmi les yeux aimés:
L'heure du thé fumant et des livres fermés;
La douceur de sentir la fin de la soirée;
La fatigue charmante et l'attente adorée
De l'ombre nuptiale et de la douce nuit,
Oh! tout cela, mon rêve attendri le poursuit
Sans relâche, à travers toutes remises vaines,
Impatient des mois, furieux des semaines!

XIV

The fireside, the lamplight intimate and low,
reverie with finger at the brow,
and eyes that lose themselves in answering looks;
the hour of steaming tea and the closed books;
the sweetness as the evening ends, the charming
weariness, the dearly awaited swarming,
in the soft nighttime, of the nuptial shadows,—
oh, all this my tender dreaming follows;
through vain delays, unceasingly it seeks,
fretting at months and furious at the weeks.

XVI

Le bruit des cabarets, la fange des trottoirs,
Les platanes déchus s'effeuillant dans l'air noir,
L'omnibus, ouragan de ferraille et de boues,
Qui grince, mal assis entre ses quatres roues,
Et roule ses yeux verts et rouges lentement,
Les ouvriers allant au club, tout en fumant
Leur brûle-gueule au nez des agents de police,
Toits qui dégouttent, murs suintants, pavé qui glisse,
Bitume défoncé, ruisseaux comblant l'égout,
Voilà ma route—avec le paradis au bout.

XVI

The noise of cabarets, the sidewalk's mire,
sycamores shedding leaves in the black air;
the omnibus, ill-hung on four wheels, rattles
and creaks, a storm of mud and old scrap-metal,
rolling its red and green eyes as it goes;
workmen, bound for a meeting, under the nose
of the cops, are puffing on their short clay pipes;
roofs drip, walls sweat, the broken asphalt creeps,
in heaps along the gutter sewage lies:
that is my route—at the end is paradise.

ROMANCES SANS PAROLES

୰ 1874 ୰

Ariettes oubliées

❦

III

Il pleut doucement sur la ville.
ARTHUR RIMBAUD

Il pleure dans mon cœur
Comme il pleut sur la ville,
Quelle est cette langueur
Qui pénètre mon cœur?

O bruit doux de la pluie
Par terre et sur les toits!
Pour un cœur qui s'ennuie,
O le chant de la pluie!

Il pleure sans raison
Dans ce cœur qui s'écœure.
Quoi! nulle trahison?
Ce deuil est sans raison.

C'est bien la pire peine
De ne savoir pourquoi,
Sans amour et sans haine,
Mon cœur a tant de peine!

Songs Forgotten

❀

III

It rains gently on the town.
ARTHUR RIMBAUD

It weeps in my heart
as it rains on the town.
What languorous hurt
thus pierces my heart?

Oh, sweet sound of rain
on the earth and the roofs!
For a heart dulled with pain,
oh, the song of the rain!

It weeps without reason
in my disheartened heart.
What! there's no treason?
This grief's without reason.

It's far the worst pain
not to know why,
without love or disdain,
my heart has such pain.

IV

Il faut, voyez-vous, nous pardonner les choses.
De cette façon nous serons bien heureuses,
Et si notre vie a des instants moroses,
Du moins nous serons, n'est-ce pas? deux pleureuses.

O que nous mêlions, âmes sœurs que nous sommes,
A nos vœux confus la douceur puérile
De cheminer loin des femmes et des hommes,
Dans le frais oubli de ce qui nous exile.

Soyons deux enfants, soyons deux jeunes filles
Éprises de rien et de tout étonnées,
Qui s'en vont pâlir sous les chastes charmilles
Sans même savoir qu'elles sont pardonnées.

IV

You see, we have to learn to pardon all;
for in this fashion we'll be happiest,
and though along our days sad moments fall,
we'll weep, at least, on one another's breast.

If we could mingle, sister-souls, a sweet
childishness with our vague whims, and go
far from all people to some new retreat
where we'd forget our exile and our woe!

Let us be children, two girls, very small,
admiring nothing and yet lost in wonder,
who pale and fearfully go stealing under
chaste bowers, nor know they've been forgiven all.

VI

C'est le chien de Jean de Nivelle
Qui mord sous l'œil même du guet
Le chat de la mère Michel;
François-les-bas-bleus s'en égaie.

La lune à l'écrivain public
Dispense sa lumière obscure
Où Médor avec Angélique
Verdissent sur le pauvre mur.

Et voici venir La Ramée
Sacrant en bon soldat du Roi.
Sous son habit blanc mal famé
Son cœur ne se tient pas de joie!

Car la boulangère...—Elle?—Oui dame!
Bernant Lustucru, son vieil homme,
A tantôt couronné sa flamme...
Enfants, *Dominus vobiscum!*

(Continued on page 108)

VI

It is the dog of Jean de Nivelle,
right in front of the watchman's eyes,
biting the cat of Mother Michel:
François-les-bas-bleus laughs till he cries.

For the public scribe, the moon lets fall
some beams, though scattered and obscure,
where Angelica and Médor
are turning green on the peeling wall.

Here comes La Ramée, the old boy,
swearing like a King's recruit,
the rascal! Under his white coat
his heart is bursting for sheer joy!

For the baker's wife . . . —She?—It's a shame!
Bernant Lustucru, her old bum,
often enough has crowned her flame . . .
children, *Dominus vobiscum!*

(Continued on page 109)

VI—*Continued*

Place! en sa longue robe bleue
Toute en satin qui fait frou-frou,
C'est une impure, palsembleu!
Dans sa chaise qu'il faut qu'on loue,

Fût-on philosophe ou grigou,
Car tant d'or s'y relève en bosse,
Que ce luxe insolent bafoue
Tout le papier de monsieur Loss!

Arrière, robin crotté! place,
Petit courtaud, petit abbé,
Petit poète jamais las
De la rime non attrapée!

Voici que la nuit vraie arrive...
Cependant jamais fatigué
D'être inattentif et naïf?
François-les-bas-bleus s'en égaie.

Back! There in her long blue gown
whose satin frou-frous and betrays
(God's blood! a woman on the town!),
in a carriage that one has to praise,

be he a sage or a miserly lout,
for money raised in such amount
is insolent luxury to scout
Mister Dives' bank account.

Room, you shyster, well-bemired,
little priest, fat good-for-naught,
poetaster never tired
of chasing rhymes that are never caught!

Now the real night comes on . . .
irrepressible, never weary
of being the careless simpleton,
François-les-bas-bleus still makes merry.

VII

O triste, triste était mon âme
A cause, à cause d'une femme.

Je ne me suis pas consolé
Bien que mon cœur s'en soit allé,

Bien que mon cœur, bien que mon âme
Eussent fui loin de cette femme.

Je ne me suis pas consolé
Bien que mon cœur s'en soit allé.

Et mon cœur, mon cœur trop sensible
Dit à mon âme: Est-il possible,

Est-il possible,—le fût-il,—
Ce fier exil, ce triste exil?

Mon âme dit à mon cœur: Sais-je
Moi-même, que nous veut ce piège

D'être présents bien qu'exilés,
Encore que loin en allés?

VII

Oh, sad, sad was my soul because,
because—for a woman's sake it was.

Never will I be solaced, nay,
although my heart has come away,

although my heart and my soul are
free of that woman now—and far.

Never will I be solaced, nay,
although my heart has come away.

And my heart, my heart that can suffer well,
says to my soul: Is it possible,

is it possible—that there can be
this sad proud exile of her and me?

And my soul says to my heart: Do I
know what wished us this trap, or why

we are always with her, even though
we were exiled far and long ago?

VIII

Dans l'interminable
Ennui de la plaine,
La neige incertaine
Luit comme du sable.

Le ciel est de cuivre
Sans lueur aucune,
On croirait voir vivre
Et mourir la lune.

Comme des nuées
Flottent gris les chênes
Des forêts prochaines
Parmi les buées.

Le ciel est de cuivre
Sans lueur aucune.
On croirait voir vivre
Et mourir la lune.

Corneille poussive
Et vous les loups maigres,
Par ces bises aigres
Quoi donc vous arrive?

Dans l'interminable
Ennui de la plaine,
La neige incertaine
Luit comme du sable.

VIII

In the ennui unending
of the flat land
the vague snow descending
shines like sand.

With no gleam of light
in the copper sky,
one imagines he might
see the moon live and die.

In the near-by woods
among the mist
gray oaks twist
like floating clouds.

With no gleam of light
in the copper sky,
one imagines he might
see the moon live and die.

Wind-broken crow,
and starving wolves too,
when sharp winds blow
what happens to you?

In the ennui unending
of the flat land
the vague snow descending
shines like sand.

IX

L'ombre des arbres dans la rivière embrumée
    Meurt comme de la fumée,
Tandis qu'en l'air, parmi les ramures réelles,
    Se plaignent les tourterelles.

Combien, ô voyageur, ce paysage blême
    Te mira blême toi-même,
Et que tristes pleuraient dans les hautes feuillées
    Tes espérances noyées?

Mai, juin, 1872

IX

*The nightingale that from his lofty perch
sees his reflection in the stream below
thinks he has fallen into the water. Though
he is at the top of an oak, he is always in
fear of drowning.*
CYRANO DE BERGERAC

The image of the trees in the misty stream
     dies like the rising steam,
while among the real boughs in the air
     the turtledoves despair.

How much this pale landscape, O traveler,
     mirrors your pale self there,
and how mournfully in the lofty leaves
     your drowned hope grieves!

PAYSAGES BELGES

❦

WALCOURT

Briques et tuiles,
O les charmants
Petits asiles
Pour les amants!

Houblons et vignes,
Feuilles et fleurs,
Tentes insignes
Des francs buveurs!

Guinguettes claires,
Bières, clameurs,
Servantes chères
A tous fumeurs!

Gares prochaines,
Gais chemins grands...
Quelles aubaines,
Bons juifs errants!

Juillet 1873

BELGIAN LANDSCAPES

WALCOURT

Bricks and tiles,
oh, charming cover;
snug asylums
for the lovers!

Hops and vines,
flowers winking,
notorious dens
for serious drinking!

Bright inns with beer
and noisy jokes,
barmaids dear
to all who smoke!

Stations near,
gay roads to choose...
what windfalls here,
good wandering Jews?

CHARLEROI

Dans l'herbe noire
Les Kobolds vont.
Le vent profond
Pleure, on veut croire.

Quoi donc se sent?
L'avoine siffle.
Un buisson giffle
L'œil au passant.

Plutôt des bouges
Que des maisons.
Quels horizons
De forges rouges!

On sent donc quoi?
Des gares tonnent,
Les yeux s'étonnent,
Où Charleroi?

(Continued on page 120)

CHARLEROI

In the black grass
the Kobolds go.
The wind is low
and weeps, I guess.

What went by?
The oatstraws whistle.
That was a thistle
slapped my eye.

Hovels instead
of houses. Oh,
the horizon's red
with the forges' glow!

Hear that, boy?
The stations thunder.
Look! I wonder
where's Charleroi?

(Continued on page 121)

Parfums sinistres?
Qu'est-ce que c'est?
Quoi bruissait
Comme des sistres?

Sites brutaux!
Oh! votre haleine,
Sueur humaine,
Cris des métaux!

Dans l'herbe noire
Les Kobolds vont.
Le vent profond
Pleure, on veut croire.

Evil smells!
Where are they from?
What roars and yells,
what sistra hum?

Oh, brutal site!
What stenches rise!
Human sweat!
Metallic cries!

In the black grass
the Kobolds go.
The wind is low
and weeps, I guess.

BRUXELLES

CHEVAUX DE BOIS

Par Saint-Gille,
Viens-nous-en,
Mon agile
Alezan.
V. Hugo

Tournez, tournez, bons chevaux de bois,
Tournez cent tours, tournez mille tours,
Tournez souvent et tournez toujours,
Tournez, tournez au son des hautbois.

Le gros soldat, la plus grosse bonne
Sont sur vos dos comme dans leur chambre;
Car, en ce jour, au bois de la Cambre,
Les maîtres sont tous deux en personne.

Tournez, tournez, chevaux de leur cœur,
Tandis qu'autour de tous vos tournois
Clignotte l'œil du filou sournois,
Tournez au son du piston vainqueur.

C'est ravissant comme ça vous soûle
D'aller ainsi dans ce cirque bête!
Bien dans le ventre et mal dans la tête,
Du mal en masse et du bien en foule.

(Continued on page 124)

BRUSSELS

WOODEN HORSES

*By Saint-Gille
let's away,
my light-footed
bay.*
          V. Hugo

Turn, good wooden horses, round
a hundred turns, a thousand turns.
Forever turn till the axles burn,
turn, turn, to the oboes' sound.

The big soldier and the fattest maid
ride your backs as if in their chamber,
because their masters have also made
an outing today in the Bois de la Cambre.

Turn, turn, horses of their hearts,
while all around your whirling there
are the clever sharpers at their art;
turn to the cornet's bragging blare.

It's as much fun as getting dead
drunk, to ride in this silly ring!
Good for the belly, bad for the head,
a plenty good and a plenty bad thing.

(Continued on page 125)

BRUXELLES—*Continued*

Tournez, tournez, sans qu'il soit besoin
D'user jamais de nuls éperons,
Pour commander à vos galops ronds,
Tournez, tournez, sans espoir de foin.

Et dépêchez, chevaux de leur âme,
Déjà, voici que la nuit qui tombe
Va réunir pigeon et colombe,
Loin de la foire et loin de madame.

Tournez, tournez! le ciel en velours
D'astres en or se vêt lentement.
Voici partir l'amante et l'amant.
Tournez au son joyeux des tambours.

Champ de foire de Saint-Gilles, août 1872

BRUSSELS—*Continued*

Turn, turn, no need today
of any spurs to make you bound,
galloping around and round,
turn, turn, without hope of hay.

And hurry, horses of their love,
already night is falling here
and the pigeon flies to join the dove,
far from madame, far from the fair.

Turn! Turn! Slow evening comes,
in velvet, buttoned up with stars.
Away the lovers go, in pairs.
Turn to the beat of the joyous drums.

BIRDS IN THE NIGHT

❀

[III]

Aussi bien pourquoi me mettrai-je à geindre?
Vous ne m'aimez pas, l'affaire est conclue,
Et, ne voulant pas qu'on ose se plaindre,
Je souffrirai d'une âme résolue.

Oui, je souffrirai, car je vous aimais!
Mais je souffrirai comme un bon soldàt
Blessé, qui s'en va dormir à jamais,
Plein d'amour pour quelque pays ingrat.

Vous qui fûtes ma Belle, ma Chérie,
Encor que de vous vienne ma souffrance,
N'êtes-vous donc pas toujours ma Patrie,
Aussi jeune, aussi folle que la France?

Birds in the Night

[III]

Therefore, to what good these sighs and groans?
You do not love me, that's the end of all,
and since a man should bear his grief alone,
I'll suffer calmly and be stoical.

Yes, I will suffer, for I loved you well!
But I will suffer like a soldier, hurt
mortally, who sleeps just as he fell,
loving a thankless land past her desert.

You who were my lovely one, my own,
though from you come my suffering and mischance,
are you not still my Country, you alone,
just as childish, just as mad as France?

[V]

Je vous vois encor. J'entr'ouvris la porte.
Vous étiez au lit comme fatiguée.
Mais, ô corps léger que l'amour emporte,
Vous bondîtes nue, éplorée et gaie.

O quels baisers, quels enlacements fous!
J'en riais moi-même à travers mes pleurs.
Certes, ces instants seront entre tous
Mes plus tristes, mais aussi mes meilleurs.

Je ne veux revoir de votre sourire
Et de vos bons yeux en cette occurrence
Et de vous, enfin, qu'il faudrait maudire,
Et du piège exquis, rien que l'apparence.

[V]

I see you still. I pushed the door
half open. As if tired, you lay
in bed. Light body love upbore!
You jumped up, naked, weeping, gay.

What kisses and entwinings mad!
I laughed about it through my tears.
Those moments will be my most sad
and my best too, along the years.

I would not see again your smile,
nor your kind eyes, exquisite snare,
nor you at all—one must revile—
save as the image of what you were.

[VI]

Je vous vois encor! En robe d'été
Blanche et jaune avec des fleurs de rideaux.
Mais vous n'aviez plus l'humide gaîté
Du plus délirant de tous nos tantôts,

La petite épouse et la fille aînée
Était reparue avec la toilette,
Et c'était déjà notre destinée
Qui me regardait sous votre voilette.

Soyez pardonnée! Et c'est pour cela
Que je garde, hélas! avec quelque orgueil,
En mon souvenir qui vous cajola,
L'éclair de côté que coulait votre œil.

Bruxelles-Londres, Septembre-octobre 1872

[VI]

I see you still! In a summer dress,
yellow and white with printed flowers;
gone was the gay moist tenderness
of our delirious former hours.

The little wife, the grown young lady
appeared, dressed as she used to be.
It was our destiny already
that gazed from beneath the veil at me.

But I forgive you! That is why
I remember, and with some pride,
a flattering picture when your eyes
flashed their lightning to one side.

❦

GREEN

Voici des fruits, des fleurs, des feuilles et des branches,
Et puis voici mon cœur, qui ne bat que pour vous.
Ne le déchirez pas avec vos deux mains blanches
Et qu'à vos yeux si beaux l'humble présent soit doux.

J'arrive tout couvert encore de rosée
Que le vent du matin vient glacer à mon front.
Souffrez que ma fatigue, à vos pieds reposée,
Rêve des chers instants qui la délasseront.

Sur votre jeune sein laissez rouler ma tête
Toute sonore encore de vos derniers baisers;
Laissez la s'apaiser de la bonne tempête,
Et que je dorme un peu puisque vous reposez.

WATERCOLORS

❦

GREEN

I give these flowers and fruits, these leafy sprays,
and my heart also, throbbing for your sake,
into your two white hands—oh, do not break
such poor gifts, nor your eyes deny them praise.

I come all covered yet with dew the breeze
of morning turns to ice upon my face.
Let my weariness, before your knees,
dream these dear moments which will give it peace.

Let my head, still ringing with your last
kisses, settle on your soft young breast;
and when the splendid hurricane has passed,
perhaps I'll sleep a little while you rest.

SPLEEN

Les roses étaient toutes rouges
Et les lierres étaient tout noirs.

Chère, pour peu que tu te bouges,
Renaissent tous mes désespoirs.

Le ciel était trop bleu, trop tendre,
La mer trop verte et l'air trop doux.

Je crains toujours,—ce qu'est d'attendre
Quelque fuite atroce de vous.

Du houx à la feuille vernie
Et du luisant buis je suis las,

Et de la campagne infinie
Et de tout, fors de vous, hélas!

SPLEEN

The roses they were all so red,
and the ivy was all black.

Dear, if you merely turn your head,
all my old despair comes back.

The sky was much too blue and clear,
the sea too green, the air too bright.

I must expect, and always fear,
you'll make some wild atrocious flight.

I'm tired of the varnished holly-tree
and of the shining boxwood too,

tired of the field's monotony
and of everything, alas, but you!

STREETS

I

Dansons la gigue!

J'aimais surtout ses jolis yeux,
Plus clairs que l'étoile des cieux,
J'aimais ses yeux malicieux.

Dansons la gigue!

Elle avait des façons vraiment
De désoler un pauvre amant,
Que c'en était vraiment charmant!

Dansons la gigue!

Mais je trouve encor meilleur
Le baiser de sa bouche en fleur,
Depuis qu'elle est morte à mon cœur.

Dansons la gigue!

Je me souviens, je me souviens
Des heures et des entretiens,
Et c'est le meilleur de mes biens.

Dansons la gigue!

SOHO

136

STREETS

I

Let's dance the jig!

Above all else I loved her eyes,
more clear than stars of any skies,
those eyes maliciously wise.

Let's dance the jig!

And truly she had quite an art
of making bleed a lover's heart,
yes, she was charming in the part.

Let's dance the jig!

But most that flower-mouth so red
with kisses has my heart bestead
since to my heart she has been dead.

Let's dance the jig!

I remember, I recall
hours intimate and trivial,
and this to me is best of all.

Let's dance the jig!

SAGESSE

1881

V

Beauté des femmes, leur faiblesse, et ces mains pâles
Qui font souvent le bien et peuvent tout le mal.
Et ces yeux, où plus rien ne reste d'animal
Que juste assez pour dire: «assez» aux fureurs mâles

Et toujours, maternelle endormeuse des râles,
Même quand elle ment, cette voix! Matinal
Appel, ou chant bien doux à vêpre, ou frais signal,
Ou beau sanglot qui va mourir au pli des châles!...

Hommes durs! Vie atroce et laide d'ici-bas!
Ah! que, du moins, loin des baisers et des combats,
Quelque chose demeure un peu sur la montagne,

Quelque chose du cœur enfantin et subtil,
Bonté, respect! Car qu'est-ce qui nous accompagne,
Et vraiment, quand la mort viendra, que reste-t-il?

❦

Book One

V

Beauty of women, their weakness, and those pale
hands which often do good and can do ill.
And those eyes where there's nothing animal, but still
enough to say "Enough" to the maddened male,

and always, motherly comforter of râles,
even when it lies, that voice! The call of morning,
or the sweet song at vespers, or cool warning,
or lovely sob that dies in the folds of shawls! ...

Hard men! And life here, savage and reviled!
Ah, that at least, far from the kiss, the blow,
were something to stand a while on the mountainsides,

something with the ready heart of a child,
goodness and reverence! For who will go
with us, and when death does come, what abides?

VI

O vous, comme un qui boite au loin, Chagrins et Joies,
Toi, cœur saignant d'hier qui flambes aujourd'hui,
C'est vrai pourtant que c'est fini, que tout a fui
De nos sens, aussi bien les ombres que les proies.

Vieux bonheurs, vieux malheurs, comme une file d'oies
Sur la route en poussière où tous les pieds ont lui,
Bon voyage! Et le Rire, et, plus vieille que lui,
Toi, Tristesse noyée au vieux noir que tu broies,

Et le reste!—Un doux vide, un grand renoncement,
Quelqu'un en nous qui sent la paix immensément,
Une candeur d'âme d'une fraîcheur délicieuse...

Et voyez! notre cœur qui saignait sous l'orgueil,
Il flambe dans l'amour, et s'en va faire accueil
A la vie, en faveur d'une mort précieuse!

VI

O you, like one who limps afar, Grief and Delight,
you, bleeding heart of yesterday who burn today,
it is true that here's the end, that all has taken flight
from our senses, both the good and the bad luck gone away.

Old blessings, old misfortunes, like a file of geese
along a dusty road where all footprints are found,
Bon voyage! And Laughter too, and, older than all these,
you, Sadness weltering in the old lampblack you pound,

and all the rest!—Soft void, all wish and will denied,
something within that feels peace, immense and sweet,
a candor of the soul like the wind's refreshing breath . . .

and see! our heart that used to bleed beneath its pride
is all aflame with love and humbly goes to greet
life, in the behalf of a good and precious death.

VII

Les faux beaux jours ont lui tout le jour, ma pauvre âme,
Et les voici vibrer aux cuivres du couchant.
Fermes les yeux, pauvre âme, et rentre sur-le-champ:
Une tentation des pires. Fuis l'infâme.

Ils ont lui tout le jour en longs grêlons de flamme,
Battant toute vendange aux collines, couchant
Toute moisson de la vallée, et ravageant
Le ciel tout bleu, le ciel chanteur qui te réclame.

O pâlis, et va-t'en, lente et joignant les mains.
Si ces hiers allaient manger nos beaux demains?
Si la vieille folie était encore en route?

Ces souvenirs, va-t-il falloir les retuer?
Un assaut furieux, le suprême, sans doute!
O, va prier contre l'orage, va prier.

VII

Poor soul, the false fair lights that shone all day
are quivering to the copper setting sun.
Close your eyes, poor soul. Leave right away
such dire temptations. Flee the infamous one.

All day in showers of flaming hail they shone,
crushed the hillside vineyards, overthrew
the valley's harvest, and laid waste the blue,
the singing sky that claims you as its own.

Oh, turn pale and go slowly, with clasped hands.
Suppose the yesterdays ate up our grand
tomorrows? If the old madness came this way?

Must these memories be put to rout,
and killed again? The last assault, no doubt!
Go pray against the hurricane! Go pray.

VIII

La vie humble aux travaux ennuyeux et faciles
Est une œuvre de choix qui veut beaucoup d'amour:
Rester gai quand le jour triste succède au jour,
Être fort, et s'user en circonstances viles;

N'entendre, n'écouter aux bruits des grandes villes
Que l'appel, ô mon Dieu, des cloches dans la tour,
Et faire un de ces bruits soi-même, cela pour
L'accomplissement vil de tâches puériles;

Dormir chez les pécheurs étant un pénitent;
N'aimer que le silence et conserver pourtant
Le temps si grand dans la patience si grande,

Le scrupule naïf aux repentirs têtus,
Et tous ces soins autour de ces pauvres vertus!
—Fi, dit l'Ange Gardien, de l'orgueil qui marchande!

VIII

The humble life with tedious, simple work
is an act of choice, and a deal of love it asks
to keep gay through dismal weeks and not to shirk,
to be strong, and waste yourself in wretched tasks;

in the noises of great towns to hear and hark,
dear God, to nothing but the bells in the tower,
to be one of these noises, and all for
the mean completion of some trivial work;

a penitent, to sleep in the sinners' house;
to love but silence and yet save a share
of time by exercising equal patience;

to keep plain scruples with stiff contrite vows,—
all these small virtues among so many cares!
—Shame, said the Angel, to haggling arrogance!

XVI

Écoutez la chanson bien douce
Qui ne pleure que pour vous plaire,
Elle est discrète, elle est légère:
Un frisson d'eau sur de la mousse!

La voix vous fut connue (et chère!)
Mais à présent elle est voilée
Comme une veuve désolée,
Pourtant comme elle encore fière,

Et dans les longs plis de son voile
Qui palpite aux brises d'automne,
Cache et montre au cœur qui s'étonne
La vérité comme une étoile.

Elle dit, la voix reconnue,
Que le bonté c'est notre vie,
Que de la haine et de l'envie
Rien ne reste, la mort venue.

(Continued on page 150)

XVI

Listen to this music sweet,
weeping but for your delight;
on moss the water's quivering flight
is as nimble and discreet!

The voice was known to you (and dear!),
but it has been veiled of late
like a widow desolate,
yet it still is proud, like her,

and in the long folds of the veil
which trembles as the autumn blows,
unto the heart astounded shows
truth's star, now hidden, now revealed.

It says, this voice now known again,
that goodness is the goal of life,
that of our hate and envious strife,
past death, nothing shall remain.

(Continued on page 151)

149

Elle parle aussi de la gloire
D'être simple sans plus attendre,
Et de noces d'or et du tendre
Bonheur d'une paix sans victoire.

Accueillez la voix qui persiste
Dans son naïf épithalame.
Allez, rien n'est meilleur à l'âme
Que de faire une âme moins triste!

Elle est en peine et de passage
L'âme qui souffre sans colère.
Et comme sa morale est claire!...
Écoutez la chanson bien sage.

XVI—*Continued*

It says that in simplicity,
expecting nothing, glory lies,
in golden weddings and the wise
peace not won by victory.

Welcome this voice that sustains
artlessly its marriage-song.
Nothing makes the soul more strong
than to soothe a soul in pain.

The soul that calmly bears its wrong
is but in durance and in passage.
It is lucid, like its message! ...
Heed the wisdom of this song.

XVII

Les chères mains qui furent miennes,
Toutes petites, toutes belles,
Après ces méprises mortelles
Et toutes ces choses païennes,

Après les rades et les grèves,
Et les pays et les provinces,
Royales mieux qu'au temps des princes,
Les chères mains m'ouvrent les rêves.

Mains en songe, mains sur mon âme,
Sais-je, moi, ce que vous daignâtes,
Parmi ces rumeurs scélérates,
Dire à cette âme qui se pâme?

Ment-elle, ma vision chaste
D'affinité spirituelle,
De complicité maternelle,
D'affection étroite et vaste?

Remords si cher, peine très bonne,
Rêves bénits, mains consacrées,
O ces mains, ces mains vénérées.
Faites le geste qui pardonne!

XVII

The dear hands, delicate and fine,
hands now lost to me forever,
after all these human errors,
all these heathen acts of mine,

after roads and strands and streams,
the countries and the provinces,
more royal than in the days of princes,
the tender hands which bring me dreams.

Hands in dream, hands on my soul,
among vile rumors without end,
do I know what you condescend
to say unto my fainting soul?

Does it lie, my pure vision
of spiritual affinity,
of motherly complicity,
of vast and intimate affection?

Such good pain, remorse so fine,
blessèd dreams, hands consecrated,
oh, these hands, hands venerated.
Make for me the pardoning sign!

XVIII

Et j'ai revu l'enfant unique: il m'a semblé
Que s'ouvrait dans mon cœur la dernière blessure,
Celle dont la douleur plus exquise m'assure
D'une mort désirable en un jour consolé.

La bonne flèche aiguë et sa fraîcheur qui dure!
En ces instants choisis elles ont éveillé
Les rêves un peu lourds du scrupule ennuyé,
Et tout mon sang crétien chanta la Chanson pure.

J'entends encor, je vois encor! Loi du devoir
Si douce! Enfin je sais ce qu'est entendre et voir,
J'entends, je vois toujours! Voix des bonnes pensées,

Innocence, avenir! Sage et silencieux,
Que je vais vous aimer, vous un instant pressées,
Belles petites mains qui fermerez nos yeux!

XVIII

I've seen again the one child, and endured
the opening of the heart's last wound. Oh, may
such exquisite agony have well assured
a goodly death upon a solaced day.

The kind sharp arrow and its coolness long
lasting! In such instants dreams awakened,
a little heavy with scruples long unshaken,
and all my pious blood sang the pure Song.

I hear again, I see again! Sweet law
of duty! I know at last what it is to hear
and see. I listen, I see always. Oh, clear

voice of good thoughts and hope! Silent and wise,
how I shall love you, little hands I saw
but for a moment, and which shall close our eyes!

[Livre III]

❦

III

L'espoir luit comme un brin de paille dans l'étable.
Que crains-tu de la guêpe ivre de son vol fou?
Vois, le soleil toujours poudroie à quelque trou.
Que ne t'endormais-tu, le coude sur la table?

Pauvre âme pâle, au moins cette eau du puits glacé,
Bois-la. Puis dors après. Allons, tu vois, je reste,
Et je dorloterai les rêves de ta sieste,
Et tu chantonneras comme un enfant bercé.

Midi sonne. De grâce, éloignez-vous, madame.
Il dort. C'est étonnant comme les pas de femme
Résonnent au cerveau des pauvres malheureux.

Midi sonne. J'ai fait arroser dans la chambre.
Va, dors! L'espoir luit comme un caillou dans un creux.
Ah! quand refleuriront les roses de septembre!

❀

III

Hope shines like a wisp of straw in the stable.
Are you afraid of the drunken wasp's mad flight?
See, through a chink the sun makes dust-motes bright.
Didn't you doze, with elbows on the table?

At least, poor soul, a drink from this cold well.
There, now. You see, I'm staying with you. Soon
you'll sleep and I will lull your dreams until,
like a rocked child, you babble your own tune.

Noon strikes. Please leave us, madam. Now he sleeps.
It is surprising how a woman's steps
ring in the brains of poor unhappy men.

Noon strikes. I've sprinkled water in the room.
Sleep. Hope shines like a flint in a cavern's gloom.
Ah, when will September's roses bloom again?

IV

Je suis venu, calme orphelin,
Riche de mes seuls yeux tranquilles,
Vers les hommes des grandes villes:
Ils ne m'ont pas trouvé malin.

A vingt ans un trouble nouveau
Sous le nom d'amoureuses flammes
M'a fait trouver belles les femmes:
Elles ne m'ont pas trouvé beau.

Bien que sans patrie et sans roi
Et très brave ne l'étant guère,
J'ai voulu mourir à la guerre:
La mort n'a pas voulu de moi.

Suis-je né trop tôt ou trop tard?
Qu'est-ce que je fais en ce monde?
O vous tous, ma peine est profonde:
Priez pour le pauvre Gaspard!

IV

Kaspar Hauser sings:

A quiet orphan, I came forth,
rich only in my tranquil eyes,
to men of the great towns of earth:
they've found me neither shrewd nor wise.

When I was twenty a new care,
the flames of love, set me aglow,
and I thought every woman fair:
but they have not found me so.

Although not being brave at all,
with neither king nor country, I
yet wished in some great war to die:
but death passed up a thing so small.

Born too early or too late,
what have I on this earth to do?
My misery is deep and great:
pray for poor Kaspar, all of you!

V

Un grand sommeil noir
Tombe sur ma vie:
Dormez, tout espoir,
Dormez, toute envie!

Je ne vois plus rien,
Je perds la mémoire
Du mal et du bien...
O la triste histoire!

Je suis un berceau
Qu'une main balance
Au creux d'un caveau:
Silence, silence!

V

Black slumber deep
falls on my life:
all hope, sleep!
sleep, all strife!

I have lost sight,
all memories fail
of wrong and right . . .
oh, dismal tale!

I'm a cradle which
a hand holds balanced
on the edge of a ditch:
silence, silence!

VI

Le ciel est, par-dessus le toit,
    Si bleu, si calme!
Un arbre, par-dessus le toit
    Berce sa palme.

La cloche dans le ciel qu'on voit
    Doucement tinte.
Un oiseau sur l'arbre qu'on voit
    Chante sa plainte.

Mon Dieu, mon Dieu, la vie est là,
    Simple et tranquille.
Cette paisible rumeur-là
    Vient de la ville.

—Qu'as-tu fait, ô toi que voilà
    Pleurant sans cesse,
Dis, qu'as-tu fait, toi que voilà,
    De ta jeunesse?

VI

The sky, above the roof,
    is so blue and deep!
A tree, above the roof,
    is rocked to sleep.

The bell in the sky one sees
    softly rings.
A bird in the tree one sees
    plaintively sings.

Dear God, dear God, life's there,
    tranquil and sweet.
That peaceful murmur there
    comes from the street.

—What have you done, you there
    who weep always,
oh, what have you done, you there,
    with your young days?

X

La tristesse, langueur du corps humain
M'attendrissent, me fléchissent, m'apitoient,
Ah! surtout quand des sommeils noirs le foudroient.
Quand les draps zèbrent la peau, foulent la main!

Et que mièvre dans la fièvre du demain,
Tiède encor du bain de sueur qui décroît,
Comme un oiseau qui grelotte sous un toit!
Et les pieds, toujours douloureux du chemin,

Et le sein, marqué d'un double coup de poing,
Et la bouche, une blessure rouge encor,
Et la chair frémissante, frêle décor,

Et les yeux, les pauvres yeux si beaux où point
La douleur de voir encore du fini!...
Triste corps! Combien faible et combien puni!

X

The body's melancholy and weariness,
how they have touched my pity and made me weep.
But most, ah, when the heavy covers oppress
the hands and zebra the skin in the black sleep!

And how feeble in the fever of tomorrow,
chill yet from the drying sweat-bath of today,
as underneath the eave a shivering sparrow!
How the feet still ache from the long highway,

and the breast a fist has bruised with a double blow,
the mouth bleeding still, an open wound,
the quivering flesh, a vain and fragile show,

and the eyes, poor lovely eyes that have surmised
the sorrow of looking always toward the end! . . .
Poor flesh! So helpless and so much chastised!

XV

La mer est plus belle
Que les cathédrales,
Nourrice fidèle,
Berceuse de râles,
La mer qui prie
La Vierge Marie!

Elle a tous les dons
Terribles et doux.
J'entends ses pardons
Gronder ses courroux.
Cette immensité
N'a rien d'entêté.

O! si patiente,
Même quand méchante!
Un souffle ami hante
La vague, et nous chante:
«Vous sans espérance,
Mourez sans souffrance!»

Et puis sous les cieux
Qui s'y rient plus clairs,
Elle a des airs bleus,
Roses, gris et verts...
Plus belle que tous,
Meilleure que nous!

XV

More beautiful
than cathedrals high,
nurse ever faithful,
death's lullaby,
is the sea which prays
to Mary always!

She has all guerdons,
both tender and dire.
I hear her pardons
rumbling with ire.
This immensity
has no obstinacy.

Oh, so forbearing,
but also malicious!
A gentle breath, faring
the waves, sings unto us:
"You, hoping in vain,
die without pain!"

Then under skies gay
and clearer, she goes
in hues green or gray,
azure or rose . . .
most lovely is she,
far better than we!

XX

C'est la fête du blé, c'est la fête du pain
Aux chers lieux d'autrefois revus après ces choses!
Tout bruit, la nature et l'homme, dans un bain
De lumière si blanc que les ombres sont roses.

L'or des pailles s'effondre au vol siffleur des faux
Dont l'éclair plonge, et va luire, et se réverbère.
La plaine, tout au loin couverte de travaux,
Change de face à chaque instant, gaie et sévère.

Tout halète, tout n'est qu'effort et mouvement
Sous le soleil, tranquille auteur des moissons mûres,
Et qui travaille encore imperturbablement
A gonfler, à sucrer là-bas les grappes sures.

Travaille, vieux soleil, pour le pain et le vin,
Nourris l'homme du lait de la terre, et lui donne
L'honnête verre où rit un peu d'oubli divin.
Moissonneurs, vendangeurs, là-bas! votre heure est bonne!

Car sur la fleur des pains et sur la fleur des vins,
Fruit de la force humaine en tous lieux répartie,
Dieu moissonne, et vendange, et dispose à ses fins
La Chair et le Sang pour le calice et l'hostie!

XX

This is the feast of bread, the feast of wheat,
in these spots seen again, beloved of old!
Man and nature are busy where light beats
so white it turns the shadows rosy gold.

The yellow straw sinks to the whistling flight
of scythes whose lightning smites, gleams, strikes again.
Teeming with labor, all the distant plain
changes each instant, now austere, now bright.

All is a breathless straining and a stir
under the sun, calm ripener of wheat,
impassive and eternal laborer
who plumps the sour grapes and makes them sweet.

Work, old sun, work for the bread and wine,
feed man with the milk of earth, and pour
the honest glass in which laughs the divine
oblivion. Harvesters, vintners, this is your hour!

From the wine's fire and the virtue of the grain,
the fruit of man's strength spread to earth's far posts,
God reaps, gathers the vintage, and ordains
to his ends Blood for the chalice, Flesh for the host!

JADIS ET NAGUÈRE

1884

JADIS

PIERROT

Ce n'est plus le rêveur lunaire du vieil air
Qui riait aux aïeux dans les dessus de portes;
Sa gaîté, comme sa chandelle, hélas! est morte,
Et son spectre aujourd'hui nous hante, mince et clair.

Et voici que parmi l'effroi d'un long éclair
Sa pâle blouse a l'air, au vent froid que l'emporte,
D'un linceul, et sa bouche est béante, de sorte
Qu'il semble hurler sous les morsures du ver.

Avec le bruit d'un vol d'oiseaux de nuit qui passe,
Ses manches blanches font vaguement par l'espace
Des signes fous auxquels personne ne répond.

Ses yeux sont deux grands trous où rampe du phosphore,
Et la farine rend plus effroyable encore
Sa face exsangue au nez pointu de moribond.

JADIS

❦

PIERROT

This is no moonstruck dreamer from the play
who jeered at pictures of his dead grandsires;
his light heart, like his candle, has lost its fire—
his thin transparent ghost haunts us today.

See, in the terror of the lightning-flash
his pale blouse, on the cold wind, has the shape
of a long winding-sheet, his mouth's agape
and seems to howl while the worms gnaw his flesh.

With the sound of wing-flaps of some bird at night,
his white sleeves signal foolishly through space
to someone unknown who does not reply.

His eyes are holes of phosphorescent light,
and the flour makes more awful the bloodless face
with the pointed nose of one about to die.

KALÉIDOSCOPE

Dans une rue, au cœur d'une ville de rêve,
Ce sera comme quand on a déjà vécu:
Un instant à la fois très vague et très aigu...
O ce soleil parmi la brume qui se lève!

O ce cri sur la mer, cette voix dans les bois!
Ce sera comme quand on ignore des causes:
Un lent réveil après bien des métempsycoses:
Les choses seront plus les mêmes qu'autrefois

Dans cette rue, au cœur de la ville magique
Où des orgues moudront des gigues dans les soirs,
Où les cafés auront des chats sur les dressoirs,
Et que traverseront des bandes de musique.

Ce sera si fatal qu'on en croira mourir:
Des larmes ruisselant douces le long des joues,
Des rires sanglotés dans le fracas des roues,
Des invocations à la mort de venir,

(Continued on page 176)

KALEIDOSCOPE

In a street, in the heart of a city of dreams,
it will be as if one had lived there in past years:
an instant at once very vague, very clear . . .
Oh, this sun shining through a fog rising in steam!

Oh, this voice in the woods, this cry on the sea!
It will be as if one had forgotten the causes:
he slowly wakes up from these metempsychoses,
and things will be then as they all used to be

in this street, in the heart of the magical town
when the organ grinds jigs for the ends of the days,
where the inns will have cats sleeping on the buffets,
and bands of musicians stroll up and stroll down.

It will be so inevitable, one almost feels
he'll die of it, while down his cheeks roll the tears,
and the laughter sobbed out in the fracas of the wheels,
invocations to death that will come with the years,

(Continued on page 177)

175

KALÉIDOSCOPE—*Continued*

Des mots anciens comme des bouquets de fleurs fanées!
Les bruits aigres des bals publics arriveront,
Et des veuves avec du cuivre après leur front,
Paysannes, fendront la foule des traîneés

Qui flânent là, causant avec d'affreux moutards
Et des vieux sans sourcils que la dartre enfarine,
Cependant qu'à deux pas, dans des senteurs d'urine,
Quelque fête publique enverra des pétards.

Ce sera comme quand on rêve et qu'on s'éveille!
Et que l'on se rendort et que l'on rêve encor
De la même féerie et du même décor,
L'été, dans l'herbe, au bruit moiré d'un vol d'abeille.

with out-of-date words like bouquets of dried flowers!
From public dance-halls will come the shrill sounds,
and widows whose foreheads the sun has burned brown,
peasants, will push through the crowd of young whores

who saunter there, chatting with frightful blackguards
and old men without eyebrows, with dandruff for powder,
while not two steps away, in the urinals' odor,
for some public fête they'll be firing petards.

It will be just like dreams when one wakes up to see
what's doing, then falls asleep, dreaming once more
of the same old enchantment, the same old décor,
summer, grass, the moiré of the buzz of a bee.

A HORATIO

Ami, le temps n'est plus des guitares, des plumes,
Des créanciers, des duels hilares à propos
De rien, des cabarets, des pipes aux chapeaux
Et de cette gaîté banale où nous nous plûmes.

Voici venir, ami très tendre, qui t'allumes
Au moindre dé pipé, mon doux briseur de pots,
Horatio, terreur et gloire des tripots,
Cher diseur de jurons à remplir cent volumes,

Voici venir parmi les brumes d'Elseneur
Quelque chose de moins plaisant, sur mon honneur,
Qu'Ophélia, l'enfant aimable qui s'étonne.

C'est le spectre, le spectre impérieux! Sa main
Montre un but et son œil éclaire et son pied tonne,
Hélas! et nul moyen de remettre à demain!

TO HORATIO

My friend, it's no time now for plumes, for loud
guitars, for creditors, hilarious brawls
over nothing, taverns, long clay pipes—for all
this vulgar fun of which we were so proud.

Here comes, my dear friend, one you will not gull
at all with loaded dice, my fine pot-breaker,
Horatio, the leaping-house's glory and terror,
with oaths to make a hundred volumefuls.

See there! Strides through the fogs of Elsinore
something far less charming, understand,
than sweet Ophelia, girl with eyes of wonder.

The specter, the implacable! His hand
points *finis,* eyes dart lightning, his feet thunder,
zounds! and he can't be put off any more.

ART POÉTIQUE

De la musique avant toute chose,
Et pour cela préfère l'Impair
Plus vague et plus soluble dans l'air,
Sans rien en lui qui pèse ou qui pose.

Il faut aussi que tu n'ailles point
Choisir tes mots sans quelque méprise:
Rien de plus cher que la chanson grise
Où l'Indécis au Précis se joint.

C'est des beaux yeux derrière les voiles,
C'est le grand jour tremblant de midi,
C'est, par un ciel d'automne attiédi,
Le bleu fouillis des claires étoiles!

Car nous voulons la Nuance encor,
Pas la Couleur, rien que la nuance!
Oh! la nuance seule fiance
Le rêve au rêve et la flûte au cor!

Fuis du plus loin la Pointe assassine,
L'Esprit cruel et le rire impur,
Qui font pleurer les yeux de l'Azur,
Et tout cet ail de basse cuisine!

(Continued on page 182)

THE ART OF POETRY

You must have music first of all,
and for that a rhythm uneven is best,
vague in the air and soluble,
with nothing heavy and nothing at rest.

You must not scorn to do some wrong
in choosing the words to fill your lines:
nothing more dear than the tipsy song
where the Undefined and Exact combine.

It is the veiled and lovely eye,
the full noon quivering with light;
it is, in the cool of an autumn sky,
the blue confusion of stars at night!

Never the Color, always the Shade,
always the nuance is supreme!
Only by shade is the trothal made
between flute and horn, of dream with dream!

Epigram's an assassin! Keep
away from him, fierce Wit, and vicious
laughter that makes the Azure weep,
and from all that garlic of vulgar dishes!

(Continued on page 183)

ART POÉTIQUE—*Continued*

Prends l'éloquence et tords-lui son cou!
Tu feras bien, en train d'énergie,
De rendre un peu la Rime assagie.
Si l'on n'y veille, elle ira jusqu'où?

O qui dira les torts de la Rime!
Quel enfant sourd ou quel nègre fou
Nous a forgé ce bijou d'un sou
Qui sonne creux et faux sous la lime?

De la musique encore et toujours!
Que ton vers soit la chose envolée
Qu'on sent qui fuit d'une âme en allée
Vers d'autres cieux è d'autres amours.

Que ton vers soit la bonne aventure
Éparse au vent crispé du matin
Qui va fleurant la menthe et le thym...
Et tout le reste est littérature.

Take Eloquence and wring his neck!
You would do well, by force and care,
wisely to hold Rhyme in check,
or she's off—if you don't watch—God knows where!

Oh, who will tell the wrongs of Rhyme?
What crazy negro or deaf child
made this trinket for a dime,
sounding hollow and false when filed?

Let there be music, again and forever!
Let your verse be a quick-wing'd thing and light—
such as one feels when a new love's fervor
to other skies wings the soul in flight.

Happy-go-lucky, let your lines
disheveled run where the dawn winds lure,
smelling of wild mint, smelling of thyme ...
and all the rest is literature.

LE PITRE

Le tréteau qu'un orchestre emphatique secoue
Grince sous les grands pieds du maigre baladin
Qui harangue non sans finesse et sans dédain
Les badauds piétinant devant lui dans la boue.

Le plâtre de son front et le fard de sa joue
Font merveille. Il pérore et se tait tout soudain,
Reçoit des coups de pieds au derrière, badin
Baise au cou sa commère énorme, et fait la roue.

Ses boniments de cœur et d'âme, approuvons-les.
Son court pourpoint de toile à fleurs et ses mollets
Tournants jusqu'à l'abus valent que l'on s'arrête.

Mais ce qui sied à tous d'admirer, c'est surtout
Cette perruque d'où se dresse sur la tête,
Preste, une queue avec un papillon au bout.

THE CLOWN

The emphatic orchestra shakes the trestled stage
which groans beneath the thin clown's heavy thuds
as he rants, with some finesse and pretended rage,
at the gawking boobies trampling in the mud.

The chalk-paint on his forehead, rouge on cheeks,
are marvelous. He orates till he feels
suddenly on his rear a couple of kicks,
then he kisses his fat partner and turns cartwheels.

They love his slapstick, heart and soul, his short
flowered jacket and the calves that fly
even when the hoots should make him stop.

But what they really like best, smack on top
his head, is the gay peruke and, very smart,
at the tip of the queue a waving butterfly.

L'AUBERGE

Murs blancs, toit rouge, c'est l'Auberge fraîche au bord
Du grand chemin poudreux où le pied brûle et saigne,
L'Auberge gaie avec le *Bonheur* pour enseigne.
Vin bleu, pain tendre, et pas besoin de passeport.

Ici l'on fume, ici l'on chante, ici l'on dort.
L'hôte est un vieux soldat, et l'hôtesse, qui peigne
Et lave dix marmots roses et pleins de teigne,
Parle d'amour, de joie et d'aise, et n'a pas tort!

La salle au noir plafond de poutres, aux images
Violentes, *Maleck Adel* et les *Rois Mages,*
Vous accueille d'un bon parfum de soupe aux choux.

Entendez-vous? C'est la marmite qu'accompagne
L'horloge du tic-tac allègre de son pouls.
Et la fenêtre s'ouvre au loin sur la campagne.

THE INN

Beside the dusty road where our feet bleed
and burn, the Inn with "Bonheur" on its sign
is white-walled, red-roofed, cool, and here's no need
of passport; here are fresh bread and blue wine.

One can smoke here, or sleep, or have a song.
The host is an old soldier; his wife scrubs
and combs the ringworm of ten rosy cubs,
talks of love, joy, content, and isn't wrong!

The kitchen with its beamed roof, black with stains,
with chromos, "The Three Kings" and "Malek-Adhel,"
welcomes one, with the smell of cabbage stew.

Listen! That's the kettle's pulse-beat, true
to the clock's tick, with its cheerful rattle.
And the window opens on the distant plains.

CIRCONSPECTION

Donne ta main, retiens ton souffle, asseyons-nous
Sous cet arbre géant où vient mourir la brise
En soupirs inégaux sous la ramure grise
Que caresse le clair de lune blême et doux.

Immobiles, baissons nos yeux vers nos genoux.
Ne pensons pas, rêvons. Laissons faire à leur guise
Le bonheur que s'enfuit et l'amour qui s'épuise,
Et nos cheveux frôlés par l'aile des hiboux.

Oublions d'espérer. Discrète et contenue,
Que l'âme de chacun de nous deux continue
Ce calme et cette mort sereine du soleil.

Restons silencieux parmi la paix nocturne:
Il n'est pas bon d'aller troubler dans son sommeil
La nature, ce dieu féroce et taciturne.

CIRCUMSPECTION

Give me your hand and hold your breath. We'll rest
under this giant tree where the breeze fails
with broken sighs in these gray boughs caressed
by lucent rays of moonlight soft and pale.

Sit here quietly, with lowered eyes,
not thinking; let us dream. Let have their fling
love that wears out and happiness that flies,
while our hair is touched by the stroke of the owl's wing.

Let us forget to hope. May our souls keep
discreetly bridled so that they may learn
this calmness, this serene death of the sun.

We rest in silent peace, now day is done:
it is not good to trouble in his sleep
Nature, this savage god and taciturn.

VERS POUR ÊTRE CALOMNIÉ

Ce jour je m'étais penché sur ton sommeil.
Tout ton corps dormait chaste sur l'humble lit,
Et j'ai vu, comme un qui s'applique et qui lit,
Ah! j'ai vue que tout est vain sous le soleil!

Qu'on vive, ô quelle délicate merveille,
Tant notre appareil est une fleur qui plie!
O pensée aboutissant à la folie!
Va, pauvre, dors, moi, l'effroi pour toi m'éveille.

Ah! misère de t'aimer, mon frêle amour
Qui vas respirant comme on respire un jour!
O regard fermé que la mort fera tel!

O bouche qui ris en songe sur ma bouche,
En attendant l'autre rire plus farouche!
Vite, éveille-toi! Dis, l'âme est immortelle?

POEM TO BE ASPERSED

I leaned above your sleep's oblivion,
chaste body slumbering on the humble bed,
and saw, as when one broods on what he's read,
I saw that all is vain beneath the sun!

What delicate miracle, to live, to be!
So much our pomp is like the flowers that break.
Oh, thought that borders on insanity!
Sleep on, poor heart, my fear keeps me awake.

Ah, misery of this love for one so weak
whose breathing now is like the final breath!
Oh, the eyes closed as by the touch of death!

Oh, mouth that laughs in dream on my mouth, half
awaiting that other more ferocious laugh!
Quick! Is the soul immortal? Waken! Speak!

A LA MANIÈRE DE PLUSIEURS

❧

LANGUEUR

Je suis l'Empire à la fin de la décadence,
Qui regarde passer les grands Barbares blancs
En composant des acrostiches indolents
D'un style d'or où la langueur du soleil danse.

L'âme seulette a mal au cœur d'un ennui dense.
Là-bas on dit qu'il est de longs combats sanglants.
O n'y pouvoir, étant si faible aux vœux si lents,
O n'y vouloir fleurir un peu de cette existence!

O n'y vouloir, ô n'y pouvoir mourir un peu!
Ah! tout est bu! Bathylle, as-tu fini de rire?
Ah! tout est bu, tout est mangé! Plus rien à dire!

Seul, un poème un peu niais qu'on jette au feu,
Seul, un esclave un peu coureur qui vous néglige,
Seul, un ennui d'on ne sait quoi qui vous afflige!

In the Manner of Others

❦

APATHY

I am the Empire in its *décadence*
watching the tall blond Norsemen march, meanwhile
writing indolently, with a golden style,
acrostics where the sunlight's languors dance.

The lonely soul is heartsick with this dreary
boredom. They say, down there a battle rages.
Ah, if only I weren't so slack and weary,
if I could bloom a bit in this dull age!

If I but had the power and the will
to die a little! Are you laughing still,
Bathyllus? All's been drunk, all eaten—spent!

Only a stupid poem for the fire,
only a pampered slave grown negligent!
Blasé, and not to know what you desire!

CONSEIL FALOT

Brûle aux yeux des femmes
Et garde ton cœur,
Mais crains la langueur
Des épithalames.

Bois pour oublier!
L'eau-de-vie est une
Qui porte la lune
Dans son tablier.

L'injure des hommes,
Qu'est-ce que ça fait?
Va, notre cœur sait
Seul ce que nous sommes.

Ce que nous valons
Notre sang le chante!
L'épine méchante
Te mord aux talons?

Le vent taquin ose
Te gifler souvent?
Chante dans le vent
Et cueille la rose!

(Continued on page 196)

194

DROLL ADVICE

Flame to girls' eyes
but look out for your heart;
fear the languorous art
where wedding-hymns rise.

Drink to forget!
Cognac is one
with her apron set
to fetch you the moon.

Let the insults of man
not touch you too far.
Only the heart can
know what we are.

Our blood's song reveals
what we're worth and how born!
Some evil thorn
is biting your heels?

Face slapped by the blows
as the winds tease?
Sing back at the breeze
and go pick the rose!
(Continued on page 197)

CONSEIL FALOT—*Continued*

Va, tout est au mieux
Dans ce monde!
Surtout laisse dire,
Surtout sois joyeux

D'être une victime
A ces pauvres gens:
Les dieux indulgents
Ont aimé ton crime!

Tu refleuriras
Dans un élysée.
Ame méprisée,
Tu rayonneras!

Tu n'es pas de celles
Qu'un coup du Destin
Dissipe soudain
En mille étincelles.

Métal dur et clair,
Chaque coup t'affine
En arme divine
Pour un destin fier.

(Concluded on page 198)

Come, all is better
in the world now!
Above all, no matter—
be glad anyhow

to be a scapegoat
for such human slime:
indulgently dote
the gods on your crime!

You will blossom again
in Elysium's field.
Poor soul reviled,
how you'll shine then—

not of those whom a quirk,
a swift blow of Fate,
can at once dissipate
in thousands of sparks;

hard metal, you whom
each blow refines
to a weapon divine
for a proud doom.

(Concluded on page 199)

CONSEIL FALOT—*Concluded*

Arrière la forge!
Et tu vas frémir
Vibrer et jouir
Au poing de saint George

Et de saint Michel,
Dans des gloires calmes,
Au vent pur des palmes
Sur l'aile du ciel!...

C'est d'être un sourire
Au milieu des pleurs,
C'est d'être des fleurs,
Au champ du martyre,

C'est d'être le feu
Qui dort dans la pierre,
C'est d'être en prière,
C'est d'attendre un peu!

DROLL ADVICE—*Concluded*

Done with the forge!
Now you'll go tremble,
quiver and revel
in the fist of St. George

and St. Michael on high,
in the glorious calms,
with the pure wind of palms
on the wings of the sky! . . .

That's being a faint
smile where tears rain,
a flower on the plain
with martyrs and saints;

that means: to stay yet
in the stone, sleeping fire,
to be kneeling in prayer
and waiting a bit!

NOTES

NOTES

POÈMES SATURNIENS

IN HIS prefatory poem, dedicated to Eugene Carrière (not included here), Verlaine borrows from his blood-brother Villon, who wrote in the ballade "Le Debat du cuer et du corps de Villon":

> Dont vient ce mal?—Il vient de mon maleur.
> Quant Saturne me feist mon fardelet,
> Ces maulx y meist, je le croy.
>
> (Whence came this trouble?—For my hard luck.
> When Saturn piled my load on me,
> he stuck these evils in, I think.)

MÉLANCHOLIA

Résignation, pp. 2–3—

An assumption of maturity wholly unjustified by the later actions of the poet. Despite Huysmans's assignment of the trick to Verlaine, Baudelaire had already done the inverted "libertine" sonnet in "Bien loin d'ici." The sonnets in this series are Petrarchan as far as the octaves on two rhymes.

Nevermore, pp. 4–5—

No matter what a Leporello list a man may have, does he ever forget the occasions suggested by the last line of this poem? Yet this is merely wishful thinking; for at this time, according to his friend Lepelletier, Verlaine had known no woman intimately, aside from the casual pick-ups of the boulevards, and these are scarcely women for whom a poet would feel such lofty emotions. Each stanza of the octave has a rhyme repeated four times.

Après trois ans, pp. 6–7—

Line 12 refers to Veleda (pronounced with stress on the first syllable; cf. Statius, *Sylvae,* 1.4, 90), a German Druid priestess who inspired an uprising in Vespasian's time and was later taken prisoner and led, a captive, in Domitian's triumph at Rome. Her career is recounted in Tacitus' *Histories,* and she is the heroine of an episode in Chateaubriand's *Les Martyrs;* from the latter circumstance she was a popular subject for the statues indispensable to the romantic gardens of France in the early nineteenth century. The best-known sculpture of her is still to be seen in the Luxembourg Gardens. The somewhat affected "gracile" was used in translating "grêle" because these English and French words have a common Latin origin.

Vœu, pp. 8–9—

"Oaristys" (ὀαριστύς), persistently mistransliterated in the French texts, means 'fond discourse.' How fresh and adolescent the whole poem is! Those lovely girls of one's first fine flush of rapture!

Lassitude, pp. 10–11—

Line 4. This notion of the mistress as sister derives from Baudelaire's "Chant d'automne": "amante ou sœur," and is also found in Mallarmé's "Prose" and even as far as Rossetti's "Sisterly sweet hand in hand" in his *House of Life.*

Mon rêve familier, pp. 12–13—

Cf. "La Vie antérieure" of Baudelaire, and Gérard de Nerval's "Fantaisie." Barbey d'Aurevilly, in his acidulous *médaillonets* of the younger poets, said of the last line, "We could wish that M. Verlaine's voice had a similar inflection."

A une femme, pp. 14–15—

Line 11. The "eclogue" was suggested by the first line of Baudelaire's "Paysage." Neither poet, however, wrote one. For the wolves Verlaine was indebted to Villon, via most of the Romantic poets, who all had a gentle touch of lycanthrophilia.

EAUX-FORTES

Croquis parisien, pp. 16–17—

Here, for almost the first time, Verlaine speaks in his own voice. The far-fetched similes, the totally un-Baudelairean cat, and the paradoxical whimsy of Grecian dreams beneath Parisian gaslights constitute a signature beyond forgery. All the words of the second stanza bear the impress of his minting.

Marine, pp. 18–19—

Only Verlaine could use such a conclusion as "formidablement." And listen to the mighty roar it makes, not to be reproduced in English.

Effet de nuit, pp. 20–21—

Line 7. Cf. Baudelaire's "Un Voyage à Cythère," stanzas 7 and 8: "De féroces oiseaux perchés sur leur pâture / Détruisaient avec rage un pendu déjà mûr..." Line 12 is from the *Choix de poésies,* in preference to the simple "Un gros de hauts pertuisaniers" in the *Œuvres.*

Grotesques, pp. 22–25—

Similar but inferior to Mallarmé's "Le Guignon." These are the outcasts, the bohemians, "les poëtes maudits."

PAYSAGES TRISTES

Chanson d'automne, pp. 26–27—

No one has ever translated, or can or will translate, this poem properly; yet it offers the supreme challenge, the shining lure of the bright impossible. Verlaine has foretold his future in the final stanza.

L'Heure du berger, pp. 28–29—

The Germans also call this time of day the "Schäferstunde," with implications of the lovers' hour. Apparently the bucolic existence was thought conducive to the tenderer emotions. After Saturn, Venus was centainly the poet's "evil star."

CAPRICES

Femme et chatte, pp. 30–31—

Notice that while the cats of Baudelaire are statuesque, sphinxine, and electric, this of Verlaine is more playful and diabolic, and is used typically to express a prophetically malicious woman. In stanza 3 I have translated "faisait la sucrée" both literally and idiomatically to show its meaning in the context.

Line 17. The marshal-duke Richelieu, grand-nephew of the great cardinal, is characterized by Larousse as "d'une moralité très douteuse." He played a brilliant role at the court of Louis XIV. In this stanza, his companions were historical Don Juans and Lotharios, much like himself. I am aware of the idiom in line 2 of the third stanza from the end, but a literal version amused me.

Nocturne parisien, pp. 40–47—

With a hebetude hard to understand, Harold Nicolson (p. 28) calls this "a long, uninteresting poem." On the contrary, it is an important piece which shows the eclectic reading of the young poet; influences are obvious. The Guadalquivir (line 11) comes from Gautier. The Lignon and the Adour of line 16 are small rivers in France—which Verlaine knew only by hearsay. For the Mississippi he is indebted to Chateaubriand. The Eurotas comes from Goethe's *Faust,* Part II, the "Classical Walpurgis Night." The Nile and the Ganges derive from his having read Leconte de Lisle's *Poèmes barbares,* 1862. The weeping tiger of line 34 is from the *Panchatantra* of the Hindus, through La Fontaine's fable. Lines 39 ff. had been written in Baudelaire's "Le Crépuscule du soir." In line 44 Verlaine forgot—or rather, remembered himself—and rewrote line 5 from his own "Nevermore." In his first published piece, he had already marked for his own such descriptions as the "railing corroded like old sous," the "rouged arms of Paris," the barrel-organ "with a head-cold," and the "quivering souls of outcasts and women and artists." Lines 75 and 76 are Baudelairean *correspondances,* and the Electra of line 94 comes from "Le Voyage." From line 90 one might strangely fancy that the poet had been looking in the Bible! And yet he has done the Seine as even Baudelaire was never able to do it. Whenever one walks along the Seine by day, where green moss drips down the stone walls and where bordering poplars are mirrored in the brown water, sometimes almost blue from the reflected sky and white clouds, he remembers the swift, impressionistic paintings of Sisley, Pissarro, and Monet, whose eyes saw also with a poet's vision and whose hands were the slaves of their eyes. This is the unconscious and naïve confession of a young poet that he was also on the way to becoming something of a scholar. And the next poem, "César Borgia," substantiates this; but I have not been able to find out what painting he had in mind. He dedicated the "Nocturne parisien" to his friend Edmond Lepelletier.

⟡   ⟡   ⟡

Épilogue, which concludes the *Poèmes saturniens,* is too long for inclusion, but it deserves analysis as a summary of the poet's ideas at twenty-two. In Part I we are given a background set with typical Verlainean décor: garden roses, autumn breezes, gentle atmosphere with sisterly kisses. To the poet comes Nature to wipe the sweat from his brow—a trick picked up from the old tale of Our Lady's Juggler—and to give his passionate heart strength and peace. This all seems quite in the tradition of the Romantics, but he is too good a Baudelairean to believe it himself. In Part II is a fine stanza: "All right, we have set forth on our quest, / and the young stallion of our joyous chase, / foaming and flustered by his virgin race, / must have a little shadow and some rest." Sired, of course, by Pegasus, and a good running mate for Rilke's white horse which had come out "for a night in the meadow, on his own; / on his neck tossed the shock / of his mane . . . ah, leaping fountains of stallion's blood!" (*Sonnets to Orpheus,* I, 20.) Then the young poet begins his attack on Romantic poetry. First, he mistrusts Inspiration, for that "makes in young brains / whole gardenfuls of brand-new poems sprout, / like dandelions enameling the lanes." No! he intends to be very Parnassian, one of the "Supreme Poets" who have no Beatrice, who chisel their words like precious chalices, and who make moving verses very coldly. To achieve this requires perseverance and will power and thus the idea may be seized, "as a noble condor / [seizes] the bison's smoking flanks, and wings off yonder, / bearing his trophy up to skies of gold!" And that is something I crave to see: the condor (supplied by Leconte de Lisle) would be a marvelously developed bird, and the bison (from Chateaubriand) would have to be very young and undernourished. This reminds me: an ornithological thesis fairly croaks for the doing—something about the favorite birds in the several periods of French literature. The Classicists loved the eagle (Zeus and Pindar) and the dove (Sappho and Venus); the Romantics were either in a tither over the hoot owl of meditative evening or the cheerful matutinal skylark, that "blithe spirit at heaven's

207

gate." This left the Parnassians little in the zoo save the condor, and Leconte de Lisle dragged him out: a noble and aloof bird which fancied living on a pure frigid unscalable mountain in the Andes. But the more urban Symbolists got safely back to the equally majestic and more accessible swan, which could be interviewed in any proper little puddle in a prim or pompous Parisian popular public park, for purely poetic purposes, by polite pedestrians—as witness the swans of Baudelaire, Mallarmé, Valéry, Stefan George, and Rilke. The penultimate stanza had already been written by Gautier in "L'Art." The whole poem is rather a mixed credo, and the book itself contains evidences of many influences; yet in several of the poems Verlaine speaks decisively in the vague voice which is to carry his memory down time.

FÊTES GALANTES

Clair de lune, pp. 52–53—

This is perhaps Verlaine's first purely Symbolist poem. Notice that the lady's soul is the real subject; but the trope makes the poem. It is doubtful that he had any particular woman in mind. The mood was probably stimulated by some gay courtesan from the canvases of the painters about Versailles. The force of "choisi" is that it implies a landscape *composed* ideally by an artist, like Watteau.

Pantomime, pp. 54–55—

The figures here, as in "Colombine" (p. 70), are from Italian comedy, by way of Molière's plays. See the pictures of Lancret, Pater, and Fragonard.

Sur l'herbe, pp. 56–57—

La Camargo was a Belgian danseuse famous in Paris in the mid-eighteenth century. All the fine ladies of the period had to have either an abbé or a marquis—or at least a lapdog—in attendance.

Les Ingénus, pp. 60–61—

What a delicious understanding of the yearnings and trepidations of young love! And notice the understated prophecy of a future still more tender: this is Verlaine's purlieu, trespassed on by no other poet.

Les Coquillages, pp. 64–65—

This is quite too cynically gay for a young man of his age to have done. Yet, *voilá!* The use of the past definite in the last line, after all the other verbs in the present, need bother no one: the poet had solved that problem to his own liking. The final shell was a specimen of *Cypraea mus*, a charming cowry, the ventral view of which is amusingly apposite. (See Walter F. Webb's *Handbook for Shell Collectors*, Rochester, 1936, p. 384.) The poem, done in terza rima, is too tricky to be reproduced exactly in English.

Cythère, pp. 68–69—

I have never heard that sherbets are particularly sustaining in this contingency. The latticework pavilions and the rose trees are appropriately of Versailles, especially around the "hameau," that group of imitation peasant cottages, still gay with the memory of rendezvous of the insouciant Capetians and their so fragile ladies.

En bateau, pp. 70–71—

This is a little "Voyage à Cythère," and the whole has been set to music by Debussy. How little the technique of aquatic parties has changed in a century! Even the "briquet" (flint) of line 3 is still used for a cigarette lighter in France.

Le Faune, pp. 72–73—

This picture so presages the commemorative bust of the poet in the Luxembourg Gardens that when one sees the statue he hears the jangling tintinnabulations of the tambourines and is suddenly aware of the ironic and lithic smile of the poet who finally has triumphed over the "evil end"; as Rémy de Gourmont has said, "smiling like a faun who listens to the ringing of bells."

A Clymène, pp. 74–75—

The verse form here is that of Baudelaire's "A une mendiante rousse," but it was certainly Banville's first. Line 2 predicts the title of Verlaine's fourth and most famous book, *Romances sans paroles*. In line 17, "almes" is a coined word, from the Latin *alma;* the Editor solved

209

this one for me. The theory of *correspondances* was first expressed by Baudelaire in his poem by that title. Stanza 3 undoubtedly stimulated Mallarmé's famous bird.

Les Indolents, pp. 76–77–

The "Décamérons" of stanza 2 refers to the collection of tales by Boccaccio about the escape-group from the plague in Florence in 1348. The very practical young woman concerned is a bit put off by the persiflage of her talkative wooer. The whole force of the poem is concentrated in the penultimate line, on "ajourner."

L'Amour par terre, pp. 82–83–

Line 9 is a prophecy of the poet's life. The final stanza was faithfully used by Stefan George in *Das Jahr der Seele,* section "Nach der Lese," in "Wir schreiten auf und ab in reichen . . . ," except that in his last stanza the beloved is gazing at the zenth-flight of the swans.

En sourdine, pp. 84–85–

I have put this poem in a meter similar to that of the original, and I hope to have kept something of the particularly beautiful mingling of love and nature in a music vague and wistful, which dies into the song of the nightingale. This typically masculine plea for silence and concentration is heartily reëchoed in Baudelaire's "Semper Idem": "Et, bien que votre voix soit douce, taisez-vous!" and in his "Sonnet d'automne": "Sois charmante et tais-toi!" as well as by "Rondel" II of Mallarmé, where we find:

> Si tu veux nous nous aimerons
> Avec tes lèvres sans le dire
> Cette rose ne l'interromps
> Qu'à verser un silence pire.

And remember the stern injunction of Father Shandy when his wife asked him if he had wound the clock!

Colloque sentimental, pp. 86–87–

A proper obsequy for the finale of this charming book of lifeless mimes. It was Arthur Symons' translation of "avoines folles" as "dead weeds" (line 15) that started me on this work, around 1919. Bless the man! The odd thing about it all is that Verlaine was writing here something approximating what Mathilde Mauté probably told him a few years later. His treatment in this book started out to be objective, impersonal, and *parnassien,* but he simply couldn't keep himself out of his poetry.

LA BONNE CHANSON

In this book, writes Francis Carco, Verlaine "preserved so much freshness, charm, and penetration which he had imagined concerning married life, that he had created a disproportionate image to which he could never attain."

III, pp. 90–91—

A memory of the first meeting of Mathilde Mauté with her future husband. She was a shy schoolgirl of sixteen. He proposed to her half-brother for her hand within a week's time. Fast work for France of the 'seventies!

V, pp. 92–93—

This is an experiment in antiphony or a sort of poetic counterpoint in which one part reinforces the other. Read the first couplets of each stanza, then the second, and you will have two separate poems: one about love, the other about the setting afforded by nature.

VI, pp. 94–95—

The original of this poem is perfect in its tender suspension on the brink—and it is, of course, absolutely untranslatable. The last stanza seems to prophesy the fulfillment, the peace, the stilling of desires which the poet assumed he would find in his marriage.

XIV, pp. 96–97—

After his early home and school life, the typical Frenchman spends most of his evenings in cafés, and the *poules* sometimes take the same place in the social life as the hetaerae in the Age of Pericles, or the geisha in modern Japan. But already Verlaine, with true bourgeois thrift and love of comfort, wanted his own ménage. The tea is an English affectation which had made some headway in France.

XVI, pp. 98–99—

A little Baudelairean vignette of the streets of Paris. Some of the city's charm, caught in Pissarro's paintings, disappeared when the horse-drawn omnibuses were replaced by electric buses and trams; but the façades of the buildings, the sycamores and maples, the wet streets are still the same—and majestically stalking along, now as then, is the eternal gendarme with cape and moustachios. The buses in line 5 must have had port and starboard lights!

ROMANCES SANS PAROLES

This is one of Verlaine's most famous and characteristic volumes. The war with Prussia was over. The Commune was in control, and some of the poet's friends, temporarily influential, had found him a position in the press censorship. He took his new duties seriously and immediately suppressed several of the ultrarespectable Parisian dailies. With the swift reversal of fate usual in French politics, the Republic was soon reëstablished, and Verlaine was worried enough to want to leave Paris. Rimbaud and alcohol had widened the rift in his home, and the two poets decided now to have a *Wanderjahr*. The book was published by his friend Lepelletier, at his own expense, in Sens, while Verlaine was in prison, because no Parisian publisher would touch it after the scandal.

III, pp. 102–103—   ARIETTES OUBLIÉES

In line 1 the use of the impersonal verb, purposely vague, suggests that Verlaine connected the rain and the weeping with something external to himself: it is raining, it is weeping. Compare Tristan Corbière's *Les Amours jaunes,* "Le Poète contumace": "Il pleut dans mon foyer, il pleut dans mon cœur feu." The pun in line 10 is awkward in English. The indefinable grief seems more pathetic than the spleen of Baudelaire. This is one of the poet's masterpieces.

IV, pp. 104–105—

This was intended for his wife, quite unconsciously in the spirit of "You see, dear, I forgive you for all I've done to you!" But the two scared little girls hiding in the arbor—in four lines a picture immediately convincing and unforgettable, as Wordsworth's brats never are.

PAYSAGES BELGES

Bruxelles (Chevaux de bois), pp. 122–125—

Saint-Gilles and the Bois de la Cambre are suburbs south of Brussels; the latter is the aristocratic section. The point of stanza 2 is that, since the captain and the maid's mistress are off for a day's outing in the Bois, the soldier and his girl can relax and be as much at ease as they might in private. Moreover, Verlaine wanted a rhyme for "Cambre." Compare this with Rilke's "Das Karussell":

> Und auf den Pferden kommen sie vorüber,
> auch Mädchen, helle, diesem Pferdesprunge
> fast schon entwachsen; mitten in dem Schwunge
> schauen sie auf, irgendwohin, herüber—
>
> und dann and wann ein weißer Elefant.
>
> (And on the horses swiftly going by
> are shining girls who have outgrown this play;
> in the middle of the flight they let their eyes
> glance here and there and near and far away—
>
> and now and then a big white elephant.)

And there is García Lorca's "Tio-Vivo":

> Sobre caballitos
> disfrazados de panteras
> los niños se comen la luna
> como si fuera una cereza.
>
> (On little horses
> disguised as panthers
> the children eat up the moon
> as if it were a cherry.)

BIRDS IN THE NIGHT

(Pages 126–131)

Here, despite the truth of the affair, the poet wins all our sympathy. Mathilde appears, and quite rightly, as a dour little philistine, selfish and cold-blooded. The group is a sad sequel to *La Bonne Chanson.*

Perhaps this is the place—since I wish neither to make anything of it nor to appear naïve—to admit the probability of a homosexual relationship between Rimbaud and Verlaine. The sinister, precocious, and completely unfulfilled power of the gifted adolescent who disrupted Verlaine's ménage can be felt in a fragment from his "Antique": "Gracious son of Pan! Below your forehead crowned with flowerets and bay, your eyes, those precious orbs, are disturbing. Flecked with brown wine-lees, your cheeks are hollow. Your tusks shine. Your breast is like a cithara whose tinkling is surrounded by your fair-skinned arms. Your heart beats in this belly where sleeps a double sex. Bestir yourself, night, in moving gently this thigh, this second thigh, and this *jambe de gauche.*" All this may be innocent enough; but if Rimbaud was describing, as he seems to have been doing, that strange little figure of the hermaphrodite in the Louvre which is lying on his-her-its-their left side, the meaning may be otherwise. One could read, in *Saison en enfer,* "Délires": "The Foolish Virgin—The Infernal Bridegroom," in which this aspect of his relations with Verlaine is veiled with his typical indecency. In a psychoanalytic essay on the poet, Antoine Adam writes: "The examination of Verlaine, alas, is not difficult. When he is drunk, he reveals his conception of the male, and this conception is sadistic. . . . Toutes les périodes homosexuelles du poète et ses périodes d'ivrognerie coïncident." (Carco, p. 104.) A wise letter to Verlaine from Mme Rimbaud put the case succinctly: "J'ai toujours prevu que le dénouement de votre liaison ne devait pas être heureux." (Carco, p. 78.)

AQUARELLES

(Pages 132–135)

These poems constitute a splendid trio of the phases of love: success, frustration coupled with fear of losing the beloved, and the final ironic yet wistful misogyny of "Streets," I, in which he seems to be saying, "The hell with it! Let's go out and forget it in company with the street dancers of the slums of London."

SAGESSE

Huysmans, in *La Cathédrale* (chap. ii), says that in this book "Verlaine gave the Catholic Church the only mystical verses since the Middle Ages." Everyone has commented on the eternal childishness in Verlaine's nature: he is timid, he weeps readily, he is both spoiled and tricky; he can wheedle or curse with equal energy. Punished, he smiles through his tears, climbs gamin-like into one's lap, and sings so sweetly that one forgets his fundamental bastardy. From his very perversions and sins he makes lovely music. There is another explanation of the matter—and I have no intention of obfuscating the reader with any psychiatric lingo and gibberish:—Verlaine is almost a Renaissance man, with that strange duality which made it possible for him to be alternately sinner and saint. Gay or tearful when drunk, he was equally ready to pray or to attack even his friends, as he did at least twice, with deadly weapons. A remorseful convert to Catholicism, he writes with convincing sincerity fine poems of worship, childlike dialogues between himself and God, in which God gets the better of the rhetoric and Verlaine of the poetry—and yet, during the same period, he was also writing pornographic verse in which he put the symbols of religion to blasphemous uses and stressed the obvious sexual double meanings which are potential in any symbolism: witness the performance of the Black Mass. He calls himself "Pauvre Lélian," but notice that he was writing *Parallèlement* (1889) and parts of *Sagesse* (1881) and *Amour* (1888). There is an allegory in the *Gesta Romanorum* which reminds me of Verlaine's duality. A skeptic has condemned the evils of the clergy, but a priest points out to him the clear and potable water in a stream which is discovered to be funneling through the carcass of a dog; with fine disdain of modern sanitation, he alleges that the doctrine itself is unpolluted although the source be corrupted. Verlaine had two mouths, and one was scatological. His obscenity discolored much in his last six books. Anatole France has taken this dichotomy of Verlaine as the theme for "Gestas," an incident in which the poet goes to church to confess his sins, but the priest is dilatory, and finally the sinner bursts into profanity, beats on the confessional with his stick, and leaves, raging. Villon was a fine and successful criminal: he robbed a church, he killed a priest; but he wrote his way out of prison twice. Whatever his end may have been, it is safe to believe that he met it with red wine, a wry curse, and a gay, ironic song on his lips. Verlaine, on the contrary, was thoroughly unsuccessful. He was imprisoned several times, usually for assault; he never carried his murders to the logical conclusion—a slipshod craftsman! Lepelletier should be consulted for an unbiased account of the trial and the sentence served in Mons. The regular life enforced on Verlaine was good for his health; he had time to work seriously; finally he was converted and found a grand new theme for his verses.

Book One

VI, pp. 142–143—

I have done this in lines with six stresses, somewhat in imitation of the effect of many of the originals. But we have scant place in English for six-foot verses. Only Verlaine could have written the fine line 5. Line 8, which I have translated literally because I like the picture, means "to be in a brown study," but that always sounds silly.

XVII, pp. 152–153—

A final plea to his estranged wife.

XVIII, pp. 154–155—

The poet used to maintain that he had never seen his son; yet there are incidents in letters which would deny this. Certainly he never saw the ex-wife after the divorce. The last line was an unfortunate prophecy, because the son never even got to his father's funeral. One wonders if he was equally dilatory about cashing any royalty checks which must have been paid him.

Book Two

A group of ten sonnets, of which I have done half to represent his pious treatment. They must be presented here to save space. With little but a crucifix and a cheap religious picture in his prison cell, Verlaine's need for companionship forced him to this antiphony. Psychologically, the poems are dramatic rehearsals in which the poet takes both parts—always a satisfactory performance! Quite in the spirit of Augustine, he says in one poem, "God, you're crazy! How could I, a sinner, love you!" I doubt if any painter could do a convincing Crucifixion in our time, and yet how easily the symbols are revived in this poetry! George Moore said of Verlaine that he "abandoned himself to the Church as a child to a fairy-tale." If any comparable outpouring of sound religious psychology and convincing poetry has been achieved by any other convert to Catholicism in the last hundred years, in any language, it has escaped my attention. The good curé at Mons had reason to congratulate himself.

IV

I

God said to me: Son, you must love me. See
my glowing bleeding heart, my side the spear
has pierced, and Magdalene bathing with her tears
my wounded feet, my arms thus grievously

burdened by your sins. You see the rood,
you see the sponge, the hyssop and the nails
which teach you: in this world where flesh prevails,
love but my word and voice, my Flesh and Blood.

Have I not loved you, even to the death?
O brother in Father, son in the Holy Ghost,
haven't I suffered, as was written I must?

Did I not sob forth your last tortured breath,
not sweat the sweat of your black nights and drear,
my wretched friend, who seek me now and here?

II

I answered: Lord, you called my soul. It's true
that I am seeking you and seek in vain.
But, love you! See how far I've slipped from you,
whose love arises always like a flame.

You, well-head of peace that slakes all thirst,
ah, see my piteous struggles, my defeat!
Shall I who crawl on bleeding knees, accursed,
dare to adore the dust-prints of your feet?

And groping still, I seek you, long and late;
if but your shadow at least hid my shame!
You cast no shadow, for you are the flame!

O you, calm fountain, bitter but to those
who love their own damnation. Boundless light—
except for eyes a heavy kiss has closed.

III

—You must love me! I am the eternal lover,
the universal Kiss, the lips, eyelids
of which you speak, dear sick child, and the fever
that burns you. I am all these, I who bid

you: Love me! Yes, my love mounts, without flare,
where your poor love, that she-goat, cannot climb;
I'll take you, as an eagle takes a hare,
to the blessed sky with dewy fields of thyme.

Your eyes in my moonlight, night like day!
This bed of light and water in the dusk!
This innocence, this shrine, serene and still!

Love me! This is the supreme thing I ask,
for, being God Almighty, I could will,
but first I shall wish only that you may.

VI

—Lord, I'm afraid. My soul is all aquiver.
I know I ought to love you, but how could
a poor thing, like myself, God, be your lover,
O Justice feared by the virtuous and good?

Yes, how? Beneath this troubled canopy
where my heart's been digging out its tomb
and where I feel the heavens flow toward me,
I ask you, by what road you'd have me come.

Stretch forth your hand to me, so I can raise
this sickened spirit and this flesh that cowers.
But shall I have the blessèd accolade?

218

Is it possible to find, one of these days,
in your breast, on your heart, what once was ours,
the place where the apostle's head was laid?

VII*

—To compensate you for your duteous zeal,
so sweet it bears unspeakable delights,
I'll let you taste my first-fruits here and feel
peace, the love of poverty, my nights

when mystically the spirit opens to hope
as promised, drinking from the eternal Chalice,
while the moon ascends the heavenly slope,
when rings a black or rose-hued angelus,

while you await assumption into effulgence,
the eternal wakening in my charity,
the music of my everlasting praise,

the knowledge and perpetual ecstasy,
of living in Me, in the irradiance
of your woes—mine now—which I loved always!

BOOK THREE

In this section we have some real prisoner's songs. In IV (pp. 158–159)
he remembers the supposed prince, Kaspar Hauser, imprisoned when
a child and at seventeen suddenly liberated. But the poem is also
autobiographical, especially so far as it concerns Verlaine's experiences
as a lover and as a soldier. The last stanza of V (p. 160) means that he
is a child in God's hand at the edge of the grave. Howard Baker has
directed my attention to the difficult verbs of X, stanza 1, and I hope
I have finally pleased him. Verlaine's choice of *zébrer* is excellent.

XV, pp. 166–167—

Written in 1877 while the poet was teaching in a private school at
Bournemouth. The arrogance of the sons of the English gentry finally
caused him to give up the profession.

---

* [The third of the three sonnets under this heading.]

219

Even when he takes communion, he immediately translates the experience into a sensuous celebration of nature. He is really thinking more about the sun and the wine than about God. With the manuscript of this book he made contact with the publisher Vanier, who was to help him till the end with small payments dribbled out for bits of scrawled verses, sometimes stolen from the poet by his successive mistresses to get pot money. I must insist that "l'honnête verre," the honest glass of line 15, is certainly not the eyecup-sized shotglass of our American bars.

JADIS ET NAGUÈRE

Verlaine was released from prison in 1874, and part of this book was even then finished. Incidentally, Marco Polo, Cellini, Cervantes, Bunyan, Raleigh, Leigh Hunt, O. Henry, Oscar Wilde, Hitler, and any number of authors have probably welcomed the time they could spend on writing while in prison. Later the poet tried several experiments in farming, which naturally turned out badly. After the death of his mother, he drifted back into café life, so congenial and dangerous to him. Journalistic hackwork was eked out by several slight volumes of confessions, six of mediocre verse in which he repeated his earlier styles, and a book of critical sketches, *Poëtes maudits,* important pioneering studies of the work of Corbière, Rimbaud, Mallarmé, Villier de l'Isle-Adam, and himself. This gave him for a time the role of master among the younger poets. But by then he was too much a chronic alcoholic to command much respect, and Mallarmé, with his exclusive and stimulating Tuesdays, took over the influence, without at all meaning to do so. The former name of these loosely associated poets, *Décadents,* gradually gave way to that of Symbolists. Much of the ideology and technique of this movement had been established earlier by the influence of Poe's critical theories (by no means was his influence in France dependent on his weak verses), by the influence of Wagner's blaring music, and by Verlaine's "Art poétique." In short, Symbolism exalts music above meaning and, instead of talking about the immediate subject, takes a simile and works it so that by suggestion the reader may apprehend the poet's idea. Cf. "Clair de lune," pages 52–53.

Jadis et naguère is Verlaine's last important book of poems. The foundations of the major influence he was to effect had already been laid. He is supreme in creating permanency from passing moods, using the intimate, trivial, or casual to express delicately, in the minor key, those feelings, those vague emotions, which drift too easily into the sentimental or bathetic. He had broken down many of the stuffy traditions of French verse, and had played the devil with the chilly alexandrines of the classics. He vulgarized the sometimes too high-falutin diction by a healthy addition of slang, child talk, argot, and foreign words. He has been criticized for using verb forms and adverbs as rhyme words, but he certainly slew the stuffed and phony dragon which Hugo had puffed up with Wagnerian noise. The day of Hugolian rhetoric is as dead as that of Browning and Tennyson, of Shelley and most of Keats.

Pierrot, pp. 172–173—

Compare this figure with his gay namesake in *Fêtes galantes*. Line 2. The pictures are really "above the doors," but we don't hang pictures so in this country; in fact, we don't display our grandsires' portraits if we have any respect for them. Line 13. The flour was used by the less successful actors in lieu of powder.

Kaléidoscope, pp. 174–177—

I have given this poem a bounding meter because it hit me that way. The cats asleep on the buffets are still fixtures in the French bistros and estaminets: "orgueil de la maison," Baudelaire called them. The final line is a triumph of the Symbolists' theory of "la musique avant toute chose."

A Horatio, pp. 178–179—

The octave deals with the student days at the University of Wittenberg. Apparently, Hamlet is trying to scare his friend. The pipes in line 3 are, literally, "pipes with lids"; but I couldn't seem to manage that. Anyhow, they didn't smoke in Denmark in Horatio's days. There is a pun on "pipes" in the "pipé" of line 6. The "Hélas" in the last line simply wouldn't do in English. I have attempted an Elizabethan vocabulary in this poem.

Art poétique, pp. 180–183—

One of his most famous poems, a manifesto for the Symbolists; but Verlaine never lived up to the whole theory, for he loved rhymes too well. A French scholar—who insists on remaining anonymous—finally gave me the clue to the last stanza. One must imagine poetry, like a vagabond gypsy girl, running gaily along at dawn, singing carelessly, with "unpremeditated art." The final word of the poem is used pejoratively, of course.

Le Pitre, pp. 184–185—

This clown is not so forlorn as Watteau's "Gille," nor is he so sad as those of Rouault. He has nothing in common with the one in Mallarmé's poem, by that title, about himself. But the whole spirit of small-time vaudeville has been presented here, and the butterfly makes it perfect.

L'Auberge, pp. 186–187—

Line 10. Malek-Adhel (*sic*) was a Mussulman chieftain, the hero of *Mathilde,* a novel by Mme Cottin (1770–1807) in which Malck and the sister of Richard the Lion-hearted are lovers separated by religious differences. (The Editor tracked this down after I had given up.) The subject was popular in nineteenth-century France. A typical poem, trivial, intimate, and gay, factual and Flemish as a Breughel, with Ruskin's demand—that a good picture always give a glimpse of the infinite—satisfied. This stemmed from the wandering with Rimbaud, recollected in accordance with Wordsworth's advice. Even ten cases of ringworm—this particular variety was *Tinea tonsurans,* caused by a species of *Trichophyton,* a vegetable parasite—do not deter the cheerful mother. A French inn is something very different from those in other lands, certainly nothing like an English country tavern or an American roadhouse.

Vers pour être calomnié, pp. 190–191—

Carco (p. 44) believes that this sonnet was an early piece written in London about Rimbaud. It was dedicated, however (cf. *Œuvres complètes*), to Charles Vignier.

Langueur, pp. 192–193—

Line 10. Bathyllus was one of the pretty lads in the "Anacreontic" poems. As the description of a state of soul, "Langueur" approaches somewhat Baudelaire's poems entitled "Spleen."

Conseil falot, pp. 194–199—

Short lines are particularly hard to translate because the fewer words allow small opportunity for juggling. The philosophy expressed here seems to be the rationalization of a man whose life has not gone too smoothly—that is, the poet's own. It is very consoling with its wise passiveness, an almost Taoist doctrine, and it is certainly preferable to "Rabbi Ben Ezra" or "The Happy Warrior."

◇ ◇ ◇

I have chosen, perhaps too arbitrarily, to conclude these translations where I have, because the later poems are entirely too long and inferior; the effect of going further would have been anticlimactic. Now Verlaine is facing the present. He is forty, ill, impecunious, an ex-convict, a renegade Catholic, a vagabond, a drunk, occasionally a madman, and often a genius. Let us not go down with him to his previsioned ultimate defeat. Yet, as Hardy said, "One's character is his fate." We leave Verlaine here, with his brows already shaded by that wreath which is gathered only on Parnassus, and his ears cocked for the stirrings of the soundless wings of eternity, while he mutters, now wistfully, now with arrogance:

Non omnis moriar.

BIBLIOGRAPHY

BIBLIOGRAPHY

Œuvres complètes de Paul Verlaine (Paris, Vanier, 5 vols., 1899–1900), Tome I.
Paul Verlaine. Choix de poésies (Paris, Charpentier, 1911).
Les Plus Belles Pages de Paul Verlaine (Paris, Messein, 1935).

◇   ◇   ◇

Adam, Antoine. *Le Vrai Verlaine. Essai psychanalytique*. Paris, Droz, 1936.
Aressy, Lucien. *La Dernière Bohême. Verlaine et son milieu*. Paris, Jouve, 1923.
Barbey d'Aurevilly, Jules. "Les Trente-sept Médaillonets du Parnasse contemporain," *Nain Jaune*, novembre 1911.
Barre, André. *Le Symbolisme*. Paris, Jouve, 1912.
Bersaucourt, Albert de. *Paul Verlaine, poète catholique*. Paris, Falque, 1909.
Brunetière, Ferdinand. *L'Évolution de la poésie lyrique en France au XIXᵉ siècle*. Paris, Hachette, 2 vols., 1894.
Carco, Francis. *A la gloire de ... Verlaine*. Paris, Nouvelle Revue Critique, 1939.
Carrère, Jean. *Les Mauvais Maîtres*. Paris, Plon, 1922.
Cazals, F.-A., and Gustave LeRouge. *Les Derniers Jours de Paul Verlaine*. Paris, Mercure de France, 1911.
Coulon, Marcel. *Au cœur de Verlaine et de Rimbaud*. Paris, Le Livre, 1925.
Cuénot, Claude. *État présent des études verlainiennes*. Paris, Les Belles Lettres, 1938.
Delahaye, Ernest. *Souvenirs familiers, à propos de Rimbaud, Verlaine et Germain Nouveau*. Paris, Messein, 1925.
———. *Verlaine. Étude biographique*. Paris, Messein, 1920.
Dullaert, Maurice. *L'Affaire Verlaine*. Paris, Messein, 1930.
Dupuy, Ernest. *Poètes et critiques*. Paris, Hachette, 1913.
Fontainas, André. *Verlaine-Rimbaud*. Paris, Librairie de France, 1931.
Fontaine, André. *Verlaine. Homme de lettres*. Paris, Delagrave, 1937.
France, Anatole. *La Vie littéraire*. Troisième série. Paris, Calmann-Lévy, 1891.
Gourmont, Rémy de. *Le Livre des masques*. Paris, Mercure de France, 2 vols., 1896. Tome I, pp. 249–253.
Haug, Gerhart. *Verlaine. Die Geschichte des Armen Lelian*. Basel, Benno Schwabe & Co., 1944.
Hertrich, Charles. *La Poésie et le rêve de Verlaine*. Paris [L'auteur], 1945.
Hommage à Verlaine. Paris, Messein, 1910. (Tributes by sixty-six of Verlaine's contemporaries, including Mallarmé and Rémy de Gourmont.)
Huysmans, J.-K. *A rebours*. Paris, Charpentier, 1884.
———. *La Cathédrale*. Paris, Plon, 1913.
Kahn, Gustave. *Symbolistes et Décadents*. Paris, Vanier, 1902.
———. "Paul Verlaine. A propos d'un article de M. Jules Lemaître," *Revue Independante*, février 1888.
Lantoine, Albert. *Paul Verlaine et quelques-uns*. Paris, Le Livre Mensuel, 1920.

Lemaître, Jules. *Les Contemporains*. Quatrième série. Paris, Boivin, 1889. Tome IV, pp. 63–111.
———. "Paul Verlaine et les poètes symbolistes et décadents," *Revue Bleue*, 7 janvier 1888.
Lepelletier, Edmond. *Paul Verlaine. Sa vie—son œuvre*. Paris, Mercure de France, 1907.
Mallarmé, Stéphane. *Divagations*. Paris, Fasquelle, 1897.
Martino, Pierre. *Verlaine*. Paris, Boivin, 1924.
Maurras, Charles. "Paul Verlaine. Les Époques de sa poésie," *Revue Encyclopédique*, 1ᵉʳ janvier 1895.
———. "La Mémoire de Paul Verlaine," *ibid.*, 25 janvier 1896.
Mondor, Henri. *Mallarmé plus intime*. Paris, Gallimard, 1944.
———. *Stéphane Mallarmé. Propos sur la poésie*. Monaco, Du Rocher, 1944.
Moore, George. *Confessions of a Young Man*. London, Sonnenschein, Lowrey, 1888; New York, Brentano's, 1901.
Nicolson, Harold, *Paul Verlaine*. London, Constable, 1921.
Pellissier, Georges. *Études de littérature contemporaine*. Paris, Perrin, 1898–1901.
Peyrot, Maurice. "Symbolistes et Décadents," *Nouvelle Revue*, novembre 1887.
Poizat, Alfred. *Le Symbolisme, de Baudelaire à Claudel*. Paris, Bloud et Gay, 1924.
Porché, François. *Verlaine tel qu'il fut*. Paris, Flammarion, 1935.
Raymond, Marcel. *De Baudelaire au surréalisme*. Paris, Corrêa, 1933.
Raynaud, Ernest. *En marge de la mêlée symboliste*. Paris, Mercure de France, 1936.
———. *La Mêlée symboliste*. Paris, La Renaissance du Livre. Première série, 1918; Seconde série, 1920.
Régnier, Henri de. *Nos rencontres*. Paris, Mercure de France, 1931.
Séché, Alphonse, and Jules Bertaut. *Paul Verlaine*. Paris, Michaud, 1909.
Soissons, S. C. de. "Paul Verlaine," *Forum*, XXIV (1897): 246–256.
Starkie, Enid. *Arthur Rimbaud*. New York, Norton, 1947.
Strentz, Henry. *Paul Verlaine. Document pour l'histoire de la littérature française*. Paris, Nouvelle Revue Critique, 1925.
Valéry, Paul. *Villon et Verlaine*. Maestricht, Stols, 1937.
Vanwelkhuyzen, Gustave. *Verlaine en Belgique*. Paris, La Renaissance du Livre, 1945.
Verhaeren, Émile. "Paul Verlaine," *Revue Blanche*, 15 avril 1897.
Verlaine, Paul. *Les Poètes maudits*. Paris, Vannier, 1888.
———. *Quinze Jours en Hollande*. (In *Œuvres complètes*, Vol. V.)
Waetzoldt, Stephan. *Ein Dichter der Décadence, Paul Verlaine*. In: *Festschrift zur Begrüssung des fünften Allgemeinen Deutschen Neuphilologentages*, Berlin, 1892.
Wilson, Edmund. *Axel's Castle: A Study in the Imaginative Literature of 1870–1930*. New York, Scribner's, 1931.